GOING
BEYOND
GOOGLE
AGAIN

GOING
BEYOND
GOOGLE
AGAIN

STRATEGIES FOR USING AND TEACHING THE INVISIBLE WEB

Jane Devine and Francine Egger-Sider

Neal-Schuman

An imprint of the American Library Association

CHICAGO 2014

JANE DEVINE has been the chief librarian and department chair for the LaGuardia Community College Library since 2004. Prior to that appointment she served as LaGuardia's periodicals/government documents/electronic resources librarian. Before joining the LaGuardia faculty, she worked for the New York Public Library as a reference librarian. She holds an MLS degree and a master's in English, both from St. John's University in New York. She is the author, with Francine Egger-Sider, of *Going Beyond Google: The Invisible Web in Learning and Teaching* (2009).

FRANCINE EGGER-SIDER has been the coordinator of technical services at LaGuardia Community College, part of City University of New York, since 1989. Previously, she worked at the French Institute/Alliance Française in New York City. She received her MLS from Columbia University and an MALS in International Studies from the Graduate Center, City University of New York. Francine Egger-Sider is a native of Switzerland and is fluent in English, French, and German.

© 2014 by the American Library Association.

Printed in the United States of America
18 17 16 15 14   5 4 3 2 1

Extensive effort has gone into ensuring the reliability of the information in this book; however, the publisher makes no warranty, express or implied, with respect to the material contained herein.

ISBNs: 978-1-55570-898-6 (paper); 978-1-55570-970-9 (PDF). For more information on digital formats, visit the ALA Store at alastore.ala.org and select eEditions.

Library of Congress Cataloging-in-Publication Data

Devine, Jane, 1947–
    Going beyond Google again : strategies for using and teaching the Invisible
    Web / Jane Devine and Francine Egger-Sider.
        pages   cm
    Includes bibliographical references and index.
    ISBN 978-1-55570-898-6
    1. Invisible Web. 2. Invisible Web—Study and teaching. 3. Internet searching.
    4. Database searching. I. Egger-Sider, Francine. II. Title.
    ZA4237.D43 2014
    025.0425—dc23   2013010867

Book design by Kimberly Thornton in Brandon Grotesque and Mercury.
Cover image © agsandrew/Shutterstock, Inc.

♾ This paper meets the requirements of ANSI/NISO Z39.48-1992 (Permanence of Paper).

CONTENTS

FIGURES AND TABLES

FIGURES

TABLES

PREFACE

Where is the knowledge we have lost in information?
T. S. Eliot, Choruses from *The Rock*

A knowledge society drowning in an information sea.
Randall McClure, "WritingResearchWriting: The Semantic Web
and the Future of the Research Project" (2011)

AS THE INFORMATION WORLD GROWS MORE COMPLEX, WITH MORE PAR-
ticipants, more content, more formats, and more means of access, it sometimes seems that something is indeed lost along the way: valuable resources
are obscured by information overload; skills needed to find these resources
and to sort out the wheat from the chaff need constant sharpening; the shifting nature of search results challenge the human need for a stable knowledge
base. But the information world is hardly limited to the random sources and
search results of variable quality available to all via Google and the rest of
the free web. There is also something called the Invisible Web (also known
as the Deep Web), a huge repository of resources, admittedly less accessible
and harder to find but richly rewarding to searchers who make the effort.
Experts who have helped document the Invisible Web—Chris Sherman and
Gary Price, Paul Pedley, Michael Bergman, and others—have always identified it as encompassing valuable research resources. Even Google repre-
sentatives have stated that the Invisible Web "has been acknowledged as a
significant gap in the coverage of search engines" (Halevy and Madhavan
2009). Yet the present authors have noted a general decline in awareness
about the Invisible Web. Those who do know about and regularly use it

tend to be information or computer technology specialists. What, then, is the importance of the Invisible Web in today's information world?

In 2009, we wrote *Going Beyond Google: The Invisible Web in Learning and Teaching*, a book concerned with introducing, especially to students, the wealth of information resources found in the Invisible Web. As in our earlier book, we think that teaching about the Invisible Web should be a requirement for information literacy education in the twenty-first century. This new book builds on that previous work, while trying to be more than just an updated version. It hopes to answer questions about whether the Invisible Web is still relevant not only to student research but also to everyday life research. Is the Invisible Web, with its rich array of information resources, being taught to students? If so, at what grade level? If not, why not?

To try to answer these questions, we decided to use social networking to tap the expertise of colleagues in the education and library communities. We devised an anonymous, twelve-question survey and sent it, during the summer of 2011, to educational associations throughout the English-speaking world. We collected and analyzed more than 1,000 responses. In addition, we contacted colleagues from the information world who have written about the Invisible Web in the past. The survey results form the crux of this book.

In chapter 1, the characteristics of the Invisible Web are reviewed in light of technological advances since the publication of our previous book. Two definitions are offered. The traditional, more technological definition—that the Invisible Web represents all the information available on the World Wide Web that is not found by using general-purpose search engines—remains valid. Another definition deals with cognitive issues: the Invisible Web represents resources that cannot be found because of searchers' limited research skills. This cognitive definition is a new approach to understanding what the Invisible Web consists of today and points toward a pedagogical solution to the "invisibility" of these resources. The chapter concludes with comments from colleagues who are experts concerning the Invisible Web.

Chapter 2 provides a literature review of students' information-seeking habits, similar to the one appearing in the 2009 book, but concentrating on recent research. These studies help answer questions about how the current information landscape affects students. What is the impact of ever-ubiquitous Google, of the emergence of new hardware and software (mobile devices, apps), and of new trends in search such as personalization and social media? A number of overview, national, and single-institution studies are analyzed to determine how users look for information, whether for academic purposes or for everyday life research (ELR). The review concludes with a chart of research behavior traits exhibited by today's students.

An analysis of the survey results make up chapter 3. Respondents answered questions such as: What does the Invisible Web mean to you? Have you used it in your own research? Do you think the Invisible Web should be taught? The results confirmed our hypothesis that the Invisible Web should be taught, but the survey also showed that many information professionals and educators do not integrate the Invisible Web into their instruction.

To meet the needs of students identified by the survey, chapter 4 deals with the issue of how to make students better researchers. First we dissect the research process using Head and Eisenberg's Project Information Literacy (PIL) reports and Kuhlthau's information search process (ISP) model, before offering possible solutions to the difficulties inherent in search, particularly on the surface or visible web, where most students remain. The chapter ends with a section on various methods for delivering instruction about the Invisible Web.

Chapter 5 offers teaching resources that can help convey the concept of the Invisible Web and its importance to research. These resources include graphics, videos, tutorials, and other tools and techniques.

Chapter 6 is an update of resources showcased in *Going Beyond Google*. Here, we offer an assortment of tools, public and proprietary, toward which educators can steer their students. We also attempt to make sense of the Invisible Web's many resources by considering them as a range of materials on a continuum, from popular and general-purpose research resources to those that may be useful only to the very specialized researcher.

What does the future hold for the Invisible Web? That is the question raised in chapter 7. We offer thoughts on the directions that search technology is taking; how such changes might affect users, particularly students learning to conduct research; and, conversely, how these same technological developments will affect the Invisible Web.

This book is intended for anyone who conducts research on the web—whether you are a general user, a student, a teacher, or any information professional. It is also intended to advocate for teaching the Invisible Web and including it in all information literacy efforts. In this book, you can find out what the Invisible Web represents, learn how it can be taught, and obtain an array of tools for discovering its riches.

We hope you enjoy this book and that it provides a solid foundation as you explore the Invisible Web.

REFERENCES

Bergman, Michael K. 2001. "The Deep Web: Surfacing Hidden Value." Bright-Planet white paper, September 24. http://brightplanet.com/wp-content/uploads/2012/03/12550176481-deepwebwhitepaper1.pdf.

Devine, Jane, and Francine Egger-Sider. 2009. *Going Beyond Google: The Invisible Web in Learning and Teaching.* New York: Neal-Schuman.

Halevy, Alon, and Jayant Madhavan. 2009. "Surfacing the Deep Web." In *Beautiful Data: The Stories behind Elegant Data Solutions,* edited by Toby Segaran and Jeff Hammerbacher, 133–148. Sebastopol, CA: O'Reilly Media.

Pedley, Paul. 2001. *The Invisible Web: Searching the Hidden Parts of the Internet.* London: Aslib-IMI.

Sherman, Chris, and Gary Price. 2001. *The Invisible Web: Uncovering Information Sources Search Engines Can't See.* Medford, NJ: CyberAge Books.

PART I

WHAT IS THE INVISIBLE WEB NOW?

THE INVISIBLE WEB TODAY

UST TWO OR THREE YEARS AGO, IT SEEMED A SIMple matter to define the Invisible Web and delineate its characteristics. The Invisible Web, sometimes referred to as the Deep Web, represented all the rich and valuable resources not found by general-purpose search engines, including government information, journal articles, white papers, special collections of materials, blogs, wikis, social media, and the like. We could start, then, with the premise that the Invisible Web offered valuable resources and that people needed to know about them to complete their knowledge of the world of web information. And we knew that people who had learned how the Invisible Web complemented the other, better-known web that is presented by general-purpose search engines would make better research decisions and find better search results. We also believed that teaching the Invisible Web could be easy and should be part of any discussion of research.

In our first book (Devine and Egger-Sider 2009), we treated the Invisible Web as the technical problem (or phenomenon) it was and described at some length its characteristics and how it can be understood in opposition to general-purpose search engines like Google, Yahoo, and Bing. But even in the short time since *Going Beyond Google* was published, it appears that the Invisible Web may not be so easy to define. As the information world changes, the way people access that information world is also changing, and it may be necessary to fine-tune former descriptions. General-purpose search engines are improving all the time and are certainly capturing information resources that were formerly part of the Invisible Web. They are also redefining the characteristics of the Invisible Web as they apply personalization and filtering to search results.

This chapter will review the characteristics that make the Invisible Web what it is today. Should the definition change? Has the Invisible Web changed in size? Who is using it today and why? Does the Invisible Web exhibit new characteristics that would change the definition? And, finally, should it be taught as part of information literacy programs?

We will call upon the ideas and voices of colleagues from around the world to help answer these questions. In July and August 2011 we sent out a widely broadcast survey, a copy of which is in the appendix, about the Invisible Web, to colleagues in the education and library fields. The survey was intended not only to generate data, but equally, to create dialogue about the Invisible Web. We also contacted various people in the information world who have written about the Invisible Web and asked them to respond to various questions. Their answers will inform this discussion. We want to thank everyone for their generous responses.

DEFINITIONS

We will consider two definitions of the Invisible Web. The traditional definition is based on technological issues and remains basically the same as in 2009. This review will consider the impact of some new technology developments on the traditional definition.

A more recently developing definition has to do with what might be called cognitive issues. These relate to how people access the web and how much they know about searching or are willing to exert themselves to get better information.

TRADITIONAL TECHNOLOGY-BASED DEFINITION

The Invisible Web is the part of the World Wide Web that is omitted from the results presented by general-purpose search engines. Actually, every time a general-purpose search engine product is developed, a version of the Invisible Web is concurrently created. Put another way, each search engine creates its own Invisible Web consisting of all the information resources that it does not include in its indexing. This omission says nothing about the sites that are excluded other than that they do not fit into the programs used by the general-purpose search engines to collect data and build their indexes. But the Invisible Web includes many valuable sources of data and information; hence this book is dedicated to exploring its value.

Each search engine creates its own environment of resources, and the sites that are included may vary greatly from one search engine to another. The leading search engines do duplicate many resources in their indexing, but as overlap studies have shown, they differ significantly in their coverage (see Dogpile.com 2007). Hence it is always a good idea to use more than one search engine for research. However, although search engines are always boasting about the breadth of their indexing, they say almost nothing about what they exclude. They hope that people will consider them to be comprehensive. In fact, all search engines exclude material, and those resources form their Invisible Web.

To better understand this symbiotic relationship, let us review how search engines work. Contrary to popular understanding, search engines do not search the open World Wide Web. When a user submits a search query, the search engine will in turn query its own internal information world, which it has created by finding resources on the open web and adding them to its own limited representation of the web. This is the only way that search engines can offer quick results. Searching through the whole World Wide Web in real time for each query would be too time-consuming: users expect prompt answers, and search engines like to boast of their speed in providing them.

Search engines use programs called spiders, robots, or crawlers to actually search the wider web to locate resources. Once the program locates a site, it adds it to its index; then it can include the site in search results. In other words, the search engines work with a pre-assembled list of potential results, not a list assembled at the time of query. Users receive a quick answer with many resources that may help them, but they are only tapping into the universe according to the search engine, not into the entire World Wide Web of the moment.

That might be fine if a single search engine could actually include all the data on the web up to and including, say, yesterday. But when search engine

FIGURE 1.1 Server farm

Courtesy of Simon Law, used under a Creative
Commons Attribution-ShareAlike license.

companies decide to build their version of the web universe, they must make decisions about what to include in it. They are not making decisions about excluding particular information; they are deciding what is technically feasible and what is essential to include. These are practical decisions. To recreate the web in their own environment, they have to provide a great deal of server capacity (see fig. 1.1): imagine the server farms needed to keep Google going. Remember that the World Wide Web as a whole is a shared responsibility, supported by servers all over the world and sponsored by all kinds of organizations. The question for a search engine is how much server capacity is needed to do a good job.

Answering this question entails making multiple decisions. A search engine must decide, for instance, what *formats* to include in its indexing. Older search engines cannot, of course, have anticipated new formats and must decide whether or not to add them as they arise. Excluded formats, new or old, are one part of Invisible Web.

Another decision is *how much information to take from any one site*. It is nearly impossible to know how much general-purpose search engines do take from a given site, but it is clear that very rich, deep sites are only partially represented in the indexing. As Wouters, Reddy, and Aguillo put it in their 2006 article on the visibility of information on the web, "The size of the website is negatively correlated to website visibility. The larger the website, the smaller its visibility" (113). The parts that are left out are another part of the Invisible Web.

The search engine must also decide *how often* its spider will revisit sites to collect changes, new material, and links to new sites. The best search engines do it often, but until this new material is collected, there are gaps which are part of the Invisible Web. Think about how much information may be lost if a search engine reviews the web only once a month. Important events and news developments will not be presented in a timely fashion. To fulfill the need to provide current news items, most search engines adapt their programming to review news frequently as a priority.

These kinds of technical decisions create a first layer of Invisible Web content. So far the criteria are formats, depth of indexing, and currency, qualities that, again, say nothing about the value of the information offered by the excluded sites. These are simply practical decisions. There are other technological factors that eliminate even more material from search engine indexing and create the next layer of the Invisible Web.

The largest contributor to Invisible Web information consists of resources locked away in *databases*. Databases are collections of materials with their own organization and their own search and retrieval functions. Databases often offer valuable resources that have been vetted by a review or editorial process. Search engine spiders can find the databases but they cannot necessarily enter into them for content. The spider programs used to gather and index sites simply cannot fill out the necessary query forms that databases rely on.

Not all database content is invisible to search engines; it may depend on how the database is constructed. There are protocols today whereby databases can permit their content to be retrieved by search engine spider programs, provided that each database information element has its own permanent Universal Resource Locator (URL). Such elements are called static results in that the information can always reliably be found using that URL. Many databases, however, are constructed using a dynamic structure without permanent URLs. When you query the database, a list of relevant resources is assembled at that time and each item assigned a temporary URL. When the user finishes up and closes the search, the URLs disappear. The user can retrieve the same list of resources only by re-asking the question. Without fixed, reliable URLs, the search engine cannot collect and offer the information in its results.

Google has developed partial solutions to this problem and can now include some content from these dynamic databases through a method they call "surfacing." Surfacing entails creating a program to ask multiple questions of a database and then capture the results for indexing in the Google search engine (Madhavan et al. 2008.) It is not possible for Google or anyone else to solve the problem totally at this time. Why, you may ask, don't the databases themselves adapt their own design? Many have, but such a change represents several policy decisions. Adapting may require more server space. Extensive databases simply may not feel the need to change something which works well in its own right. And some databases may not want their materials accessible through general-purpose search engines.

Examples of the latter are proprietary databases whose content is available only to a membership or through a subscription. This is an important reminder that not all information on the web is available for free. Some important sources are available only to those willing to pay for them or lucky enough to have libraries available to them that offer users free access to such products. Most academic libraries offer databases specially chosen for their students' needs and subject requirements. Most public libraries also offer a good selection of subscription databases for their wide range of users. Companies subscribe to specialized services that offer exactly what they need rather than depending on general search engines like Google. Many professional organizations offer content only to their memberships. Google is working with some subscription databases to reveal their content via Google Scholar. The limitation is that while Google Scholar can help identify whether an article or resource is available in a subscription database, it cannot actually provide the content to the user. All this proprietary content is part of the Invisible Web; indeed, any fee-based information online is part of the Invisible Web.

Some information is locked behind forms other than database search query forms and is thus also part of the Invisible Web. These forms require information from the user before they can supply information. The requirement may be as simple as a zip code or more extensive, but search engine spiders cannot fill out the forms, and therefore the information is out of their reach.

A final layer of Invisible Web content is formed by other technical factors. There is a *private part of the web* which is used by businesses, governments, organizations, individuals, and groups, sometimes even for illicit purposes. This private web is created by no-indexing protocols that can be established for each site. Search engine spiders confronted with this directive must move on without indexing.

Another group of sites that are part of the Invisible Web are those which are *not linked to by other sites*. These can be found by knowing the URL and going to them directly. Search engine spider and robot programs build their indexing by following links from one site to another. If there is no link to follow to it, then a site may be overlooked. It can, of course, be added to the search engine's indexing by request.

These traditional contributors to the Invisible Web have obviously not remained untouched by technological advances in recent years. Smart search engines stay viable by changing and offering more and more content for the searcher. And as we have seen, Google has surfaced dynamic database resources with some success even if it still cannot enter the world of proprietary databases. Newer kinds of resources remain elusive: the world of *social networking* produces many new resources, and search engines cannot always include them. Add to this picture the processes of *filtering and personalization* that may also be eliminating material from search results depending on the searcher. Personalization is the process whereby search engines tailor results to the user's usual research patterns and preferences as tracked by the search engines. If searchers do not take personalization into account, the results of their searches may represent only their own point of view on a particular subject or favor their usual sites or similar ones rather than expand to include newer, different types of materials. A user may want this kind of treatment but, in most cases, may not fully be aware that it is happening in the background, believing that the results list covers a complete overview of a subject. Users can take steps to search without such filtering affecting the results, but they must take the initiative and follow the steps needed to turn it off. Thus personalization is another way technology can limit results. Information sources that according to the search engine do not match the preferences of the user may not be offered at all or may be lost at the lower end of an extensive results lists, making them effectively "invisible" to the user. More on personalization will appear in the next chapter.

Finally, Google and other search engines are affected by *positioning*, a technology that seems to have crossed the line to the point that it really devalues search results. Search engine optimization (SEO) remains a commercially healthy field of endeavor. Organizations want to position themselves at the top of results lists to sell their product or point of view because they know that searchers often rely on only the top ten results. SEO companies help them attain this goal, which ultimately undermines the objectivity or comprehensiveness of search results. The really important resources on a subject may be buried lower on the results list and therefore, if not technically in the Invisible Web, nevertheless equally lost.

We asked colleagues who have written about the Invisible Web how they might view it today. We wanted to know if the Invisible Web is still a concern or if technological advances have solved the problems that created it.

Laura Cohen, author of one of the best web guides about the Invisible Web, wrote the following in an e-mail response to the author's questions (July 8, 2011):

> Technology has not eliminated the problem. In fact, I'd say that technology perpetuates it. If anything, the challenge of the Invisible Web has increased because Web content is always growing and evolving into ever more varied forms and environments backed by technological advancements. There is no single search tool that can search every document, file type, database, book, journal, blog posting, tweet, comment, conversation, etc. that exists on the Web. The real-time Web is not covered well by search engines. Besides, there will always be valuable content hidden behind passwords, firewalls and other protective technologies. Despite the worthwhile content integration we're seeing now with general search engines, plenty of content is not scooped up. . . . No single search tool can retrieve all the content on the Web. I don't believe this is an achievable or even a desirable goal.

Brett Spencer, author of "Harnessing the Deep Web," responded as follows (e-mail, August 2, 2011):

> In addition to web content that is shrouded for technical reasons, I think a definition of the Invisible Web should also encompass the contents of the internet that can be accessed more easily through specialty search tools (databases, online archives, virtual collections, etc.) than through major search engines. . . . Thus, even though Google can retrieve some Invisible Web content, it is impractical for searchers to find those treasures by wading through the tidal wave of results unleashed by a typical Google search. The content of most specialty resources are, for practical purposes, invisible to patrons because they are submerged under a sea of web sites.

Dirk Lewandowski, who has written on the academic Invisible Web, had this to say (e-mail, August 1, 2011):

> I do not think that in the future, the majority of IW content will be integrated into the general-purpose Web search engines. On the one hand, we can see technology advances in indexing content from databases. However, this is (not yet) applied to the mass of content available on the IW. Also, uncovering information from relational databases is best applied to full text and does not help much when considering bibliographic databases, etc.
>
> The other approach is to let the database providers uncover their contents and make them available to the Web search engines. While it is in the interest of many such providers, others may not be interested because they offer their contents for a fee or want users to register to get access to the content. I don't see how search engines could integrate this "proprietary Web" into their offerings without changing their operating model.

Finally, William Badke, author of *Research Strategies* and of many articles about information literacy, offered this observation (e-mail, July 8, 2011):

> I think the Invisible Web has become more complicated and more of a moving target. If Google can capture Twitter content, that content is less invisible. If Facebook tightens its security features, content becomes more invisible. Increasing numbers of Web 2.0 sites are calling for logins, many of them for purposes other than security (like making users a target for marketing). Personalization in search engines like Google creates another layer of Invisible Web—content a user can't find because Google has personalized the user's preferences. The only way the Invisible Web would be irrelevant would be if it ceased to exist. That isn't going to happen anytime soon.

We also solicited ideas about how to define the Invisible Web via a survey. Most of the anonymous respondents kept to the traditional technical descriptions already discussed. They mentioned websites that are not included in search engine indexing, and many cited databases as the main source for Invisible Web materials. Here is a sampling of comments about the nature of the Invisible Web today:

- "Everything you can't find within two to five searches . . . and within two pages of results."
- "Generally unavailable to the unknowing public."
- "You have to know how to dig deeper."
- "It's the next layer of information not on websites immediately searchable by Google, etc."

These kinds of responses hint at another important characteristic of the Invisible Web. Even though it has been in existence as long as search engines, very little is known about it by the general searching public. And maybe that is an aspect of the Invisible Web that should be emphasized. Why don't people know about it? Does that ignorance reflect on its importance?

The Invisible Web includes not only valuable materials being overlooked by search engines or manipulated and lost to positioning and personalization, but also resources that go undiscovered because of users' lack of education and exposure.

A NEW DEFINITION: THE COGNITIVE INVISIBLE WEB

In addition to technical explanations for the Invisible Web, there is something that may be identified as the *cognitive* Invisible Web. To quote Wouters, Reddy, and Aguillo again, "The notion of the Invisible Web is actually a metaphor that tries to account for the phenomenon that information residing on websites may not be included in the results of searches for that information" (109). If we stretch that metaphor, we can use it to signify all information overlooked in search results. Our use of the word *cognitive* comes from a study done by Nigel Ford and Yazdan Mansourian and reported in their article "The Invisible Web: An Empirical Study of 'Cognitive Invisibility'" (2006). At its most basic, cognitive invisibility occurs because people's research skills are limited by what they know and what they do not know. If they have never heard of or learned about Invisible Web resources, they certainly will not make the Invisible Web part of their research tool kit.

We can guess at why people are not familiar with the Invisible Web. Probably they were not taught about it in school when the more formal aspects of research were discussed. Searching, for many, is a skill self-taught or learned in informal situations from friends. Unless people know about the

Invisible Web they cannot share the knowledge. Search engines are generally close-mouthed about what they do not offer. And it is easy enough for searchers to feel overwhelmed by the vast numbers of results their searches do find. People might also feel satisfied with the search engines they already use, as these do admittedly answer many questions quite well. If so, why look for more material elsewhere?

There is also another element of human nature to factor into the notion of the cognitive Invisible Web. People have grown very comfortable with their favorite search engines. Even when they know that other search tools are available to them, they would often rather make do with the poor results on the first results screen produced by their usual search engine than go elsewhere for better results. This is especially true of students, who may not want to give too much time to research. Finding Invisible Web materials requires more time and the use of multiple search tools.

The overselling of the relevancy feature used by search engines also contributes to the cognitive Invisible Web. The very existence of this feature seems to promise that the best results have been found and the top ten items in the results list must contain the best of the best. People do not question how the relevancy is determined. Indeed, many seem to believe that it is their duty to make do with the top results even though the top ten often consists of commercial rather than straightforward informational sites.

In addition, many people do not know how to search very well. They do not use quotation marks to focus search results, or take advantage of advanced search features to create more complex, structured searches that might elicit better answers. In fact, people naturally fall back on their established search habits even when introduced to more effective ways. They may be aware of a database that specializes in their subject but prefer to use a familiar Google search even though it gives them mixed results.

Add to this picture the nature of the Invisible Web itself. It is not a single resource: it is many resources. No single search tool can access it. It requires knowledge of many types of tools, requiring many steps and some skill and willingness to persevere. It is accessed through directories, specialized search engines, databases, special collections, and repositories. It may require time to explore. None of these qualities make it especially user friendly.

Various colleagues who have written about the Invisible Web have offered some comments to add to this discussion of the cognitive aspects of the Invisible Web.

Dr. Yazdan Mansourian, whose article introduced the cognitive definition, had this to add on the subject (e-mail, July 9, 2011):

> To define the Invisible Web we may have a technical objective
> approach, which commonly appears in the literature, or a cognitive
> subjective approach which is mainly based on Web users' perceptions
> of search failure. According to the first approach, the Invisible Web
> consists of all the Web-based materials that general-purpose search
> engines either cannot index, or are not intended to do so. In contrast,
> regarding a cognitive subjective perspective we cannot divide the
> Web into two visible and invisible parts. In fact, the level of visibility/
> invisibility of an information item depends on a variety of known and
> unknown elements which exist in the search context.
>
> For example, Web users' search skills, their search topic, availabil-
> ity of information resources, the time and energy that each user allo-
> cates to a search task will affect the level of information visibility for
> each search session.

Wendy Boswell, the author of many research guides on the About.com
site and a book about research, offered this comment (e-mail, July 27, 2011):

> Even with the advent of new search technology, and the growing
> sophistication of Web searchers, the Invisible Web is still very much
> in existence, and is still flying under the radar of the vast majority of
> internet users. The definition of the Invisible Web—the part of the
> Web not easily accessed with a simple search—hasn't changed, in my
> opinion. However, I do believe the immediacy of Web results is mak-
> ing the Invisible Web even larger, since searchers aren't willing to dig
> very deep and search engines are serving this need. Unfortunately,
> this doesn't always mean that the quality of search results follows the
> demand, which makes teaching and learning about the Invisible Web
> even more important.

As Geert Lovink (2009) wrote, "For the time being we will remain
obsessed with the diminishing quality of the answers to our queries—and
not with the underlying problem, namely, the poor quality of our education
and diminishing ability to think in a critical way" (52).

A solution may lie in teaching more about the Invisible Web as a complement to the general-purpose search engines. We will discuss this further later in the chapter.

OTHER FACTORS

Some other factors to consider when discussing the Invisible Web include its size; how ongoing technological developments may be changing the ways that people do research, and what those changes mean for their experience of the Invisible Web; and, finally, who is interested in the Invisible Web and why.

SIZE

The truth is that no one really knows how big the Invisible Web is, and what we see offered as information about its size may at best be called guesstimates. Many important studies of the size of the Invisible Web are aging. Bergman's 2001 study of the Deep Web is still being used to cite size estimates more than a decade later. His study stated that only 16% of the World

Dark Side

There is a dark side of the web experience that, it might be argued, form a third definition of the Invisible Web; however, this is an impression that should be clarified and quickly dismissed. It is no surprise that there is a dark underbelly to the World Wide Web that supports pornography, the drug trade, sexual predators, and other illicit activities, but this *dark web* (or *darknet*) is in no way an explanation of the whole Invisible Web. While the dark web may, in truth, form part of the Invisible Web, it must not be confused with the vast amounts of valuable research information found in the majority of the Invisible Web—which it is the purpose of this book to illuminate.

That said, we cannot avoid mentioning the Tor Project (www.torproject.org), a website that helps people establish an anonymous presence online. Ostensibly a tool to help with security issues, the service is available to governments, police, businesses, and other organizations, as well as to those who engage in the illicit activities that form the dark web. A related project is the Hidden Wiki (see http://i.imgur.com/Xq7ih.png), which can act as an access point to many of the worst aspects of the dark web. While it may be enlightening to know that these tools exist, they are not aspects of the Invisible Web that we need to teach.

Wide Web was indexed, the remaining 84% representing the Invisible Web. Lyman and Varian's "How Much Information?" has not been revised since 2003. That study described the surface web as being 167 terabytes compared to the Invisible Web's 91,850 terabytes.

Here is a review of some of the more recent literature on the subject.

- "The Ultimate Guide to the Invisible Web" (2006) contains this summary about its size: "A guesstimate. Any astute mathematician with an understanding of Web content management systems, content databases, and dynamically-served Web pages would probably say between 1 and 4 trillion pages, then conclude the near impossibility of an accurate estimate, especially because the rapidly increasing number of invisible sites."
- A 2007 study by Bin He, Mitesh Patel, Zhen Zhang, and Kevin Chen-Chuan Chang, "Accessing the Deep Web: A Survey," found that Google and Yahoo each covered 32% of the Invisible Web. This may seem to be a contradictory statement, as Invisible Web resources are usually defined as those that are excluded from general-purpose search engine results. It may, however, help illustrate that each search engine creates its own Invisible Web, which will differ from that of other search engines.
- In "Deep Web Research and Disovery Resources 2013," Marcus Zillman wrote, "The Deep Web covers somewhere in the vicinity of trillions upon trillions of pages of information located through the world wide web in various files and formats that the current search engines on the Internet either cannot find or have difficulty accessing. The current search engines find hundreds of billions pages at the present time of this writing."
- Paul Gil's 2012 guide "What Is the 'Invisible Web'?" written for About.com, states that Google indexes 26.5 billion public web pages but that the Invisible Web includes 300+ billion database-driven pages that are invisible to Google. Google, according to Gil, indexes less than 10% of the Invisible Web.

All these studies, while using different values to illustrate the point, do tell us that the Invisible Web remains large and underrepresented in the surface-searching world.

NEW INFLUENCES ON THE INFORMATION WORLD AND THEIR IMPACT ON THE INVISIBLE WEB

Several newer aspects of the information world, though not brand new, represent developments that are having a great impact on how research is conducted. These include vertical and niche search tools, social networking, mobile access to the web, the Semantic Web, and, finally, personalization and filtering (introduced earlier in this chapter). These aspects of the current information world will be discussed at greater length in the next chapter, which will examine how research is conducted today. Here, we will look at their impact on the Invisible Web specifically.

VERTICAL AND NICHE SEARCH TOOLS

The number of vertical and niche search tools is growing. Theses specialized resources tap both the Invisible Web and the surface web with the goal of focusing searches narrowly on specific topics and needs. Vertical tools target specific subject collections to go deeply into a subject field. An example of a vertical tool is MedNar (http://mednar.com/mednar), which has a medical and health field focus. Mednar does real-time searching for the most up-to-date information in publications, organizational websites, government resources, professional websites, specialized search engines, and the like. It was developed by Deep Web Technologies, which specializes in creating tools for gathering hard-to-find resources.

Scout.me would be an example of a niche product. Scout.me has a single function: it helps users find information on "free-time activities by location." In other words, it targets only a specific, or niche, set of resources. Vertical and niche research tools tap Invisible Web resources deeply but not broadly and can be successful at doing so because of their limited focus. They are very different kinds of tools from general-purpose search engines, which try to cover all subject fields and all kinds of information. Vertical and niche tools are successful at utilizing the Invisible Web but obviously have limited subject appeal.

SOCIAL NETWORKING

Since 2010, the *Washington Post* (Mui and Whoriskey 2010) and others have reported that more people are accessing the web through Facebook than through Google, the former leader. With perhaps the exception of Twitter, much of social networking content, including content generated by Facebook, is not represented in Google or other search engine results. Social networking sites have become a world unto themselves, creating a new research possibility. People ask their social network friends for answers to questions, advice on how to find things, and where to look. Students may share research with their classmates. This is another kind of research method. As much of this interaction, or information exchange, takes place in the gated communities of social networking, it can be described as Invisible Web content. How it will impact future research will be interesting to watch.

Social bookmarking sites, on the other hand, are open to research, allowing anyone to query their indexing for subject sources. These sources are recommendations from its community. This kind of social building of resources also has the potential to influence research in the future.

Specialized social networks for academics and professionals who want to be part of a community and share their research must also be considered. An example is the Social Science Research Network (www.ssrn.com). Wikis, too, are closed environments, but they are gaining interest in ways that can aid research. As Joyce Valenza wrote in "The New Invisible Web" (2009), "Why search wikis? Wikis contain conference content, collaboratively built professional content, pathfinders, archived student work, archived professional work, media, tutorials, book reviews, and more." How important this new Invisible Web material will become is yet to be determined.

MOBILE ACCESS TO THE WEB

Gartner, a company that monitors the computer industry, has forecast that, by 2013, mobile web access will have surpassed access by PC. The mobile world is made up of applications (apps), which are tools with very specific purposes. Since mobile devices typically do not offer big-screen web searching, they tend to be used for more targeted tasks. Users may not want to deal with long lists of results. If mobile apps become a major search enterprise, which is likely, because mobile devices are more accessible to people all over the world than big computer workstations, mobile may very well create its own Invisible Web.

SEMANTIC WEB

The goal of the Semantic Web is to use *ontologies*, systems that establish the relationships between items that will focus results more exactly. It was thought of as a way to tap the Invisible Web as well as the surface web, but the technology is not yet sufficiently sophisticated to make it visible. It will require a language infrastructure that will take time to develop and mature. As Mick O'Leary explains it in his 2010 article in *Information Today*, "Semantic search engines follow a completely different principle than Google and its followers. Whereas Google's basic method is to measure a site's popularity and importance by the number of links to the site, semantic search engines analyze the language of a search query in the context of the entire document. The intent is to attain greater relevance by associating the query with related language, or 'meaning,' in the document" (38). Books like David Siegel's *Pull: The Power of the Semantic Web to Transform Your Business* (2009) can be very persuasive about its potential usefulness. Siegel writes that the Semantic Web "tries to make sense of written and spoken language that we intuitively understand but computers normally don't" (13). He goes on to discuss various business applications. But the Semantic Web is still a developing concept. A good working example of a semantic-based search engine would be Hakia (www.hakia.com; see also O'Leary 2010).

WHO IS INTERESTED IN THE INVISIBLE WEB AND WHY?

Sometimes it is easier to evaluate the importance of something unfamiliar by judging how important it appears to be to other people. The Invisible Web does have a fan base, although it is admittedly a more rarified group than the users of Google and other general-purpose search engines. The people who express the most interest in the Invisible Web come from various subject fields. A search of the web will find the Invisible Web mentioned among various business enterprises. Computer scientists and engineers are continuing to seek solutions to the issues of accessing the Invisible Web; Google itself pursues Invisible Web content while representing the interests of general-purpose search engines. Librarians and educators also concern themselves with Invisible Web resources, as do other specialized researchers.

To discover the relative interest in the Invisible Web among academics, we reviewed the published literature about the Invisible Web as represented in ScienceDirect. ScienceDirect is a proprietary database of book and journal content that captures an important segment of academic research. We searched the database for the period beginning January 2009 through July 2013 using the three most common designations for the Invisible web:

"Invisible Web," "Deep Web," and "Hidden Web." The search terms were placed in quotes and advanced searching was used so that journal articles only would be selected. We reviewed each article in the search results and recorded the subject field for each journal. The results, charted in table 1.1, show the greatest interest coming from the computer science/engineering world. These articles generally propose solutions to accessing Invisible Web content with the goal of bringing its wealth into general-purpose search engine results. The second largest number of results came from the library science field, which includes professionals concerned with educating users about the resources of the Invisible Web. A much smaller number of articles were from the wider business world, which sees competitive advantages to be gained by utilizing the Invisible Web.

TABLE 1.1

ScienceDirect articles about the Invisible Web

Term used	Subject field	Articles
"Invisible Web"	Computing/Engineering	7
	Library Science	3
	Business	3
"Deep Web"	Computing/Engineering	80
	Library Science	5
	Business	6
"Hidden Web"	Computing/Engineering	36
	Library Science	1
	Business	0

Let us look at these groups more closely:

COMPUTER SCIENTISTS/ENGINEERS

Each year, computer scientists and computer engineers develop many proposals for ways to capture Invisible Web content. Solving the Invisible Web "problem" must present an intellectual puzzle that appeals to this audience. Some of these proposals may well lead, eventually, to the shrinking of the Invisible Web.

Google, a company whose products have been created by its computer scientists and engineers, is, of course, concerned about the Invisible Web and has already taken various actions to incorporate Invisible Web material into its search results. Over the past few years, Google has established protocols that databases can adopt if they wish to make their content visible in Google searches. Google has made agreements with subscription database developers such as EBSCOhost to permit the listing of their references in their Google Scholar indexing. Google has also developed the surfacing method of extracting content from databases. Google's interest in capturing Invisible Web materials shows that its scientists consider them worthwhile and certainly acknowledges a gap worth closing in Google results.

LIBRARIANS AND EDUCATORS

These constituencies are on the front line of helping people with research, hence their interest in the Invisible Web. They guide their students through assignments, create guides for the user public, and give introductory classes on research. Some librarians use the Invisible Web regularly to help solve research problems, as do educators who want to encourage their students to perform effective research. Our Invisible Web survey, however, seemed to indicate that many librarians and educators are not familiar with the Invisible Web and do not teach it on a regular basis. More about these results will appear in chapter 3.

BUSINESS

The business world, although not well represented in ScienceDirect, has several reasons to be interested in the Invisible Web. First, businesses naturally want access to Invisible Web content that may give them an edge over their competitors. Information is an important asset, and as will be seen, companies will pay for research to uncover it. New search engine startups emerge each year, some of which succeed and some of which do not, but they all like to promote their tools as the ones that provide better results than the more established alternatives. The successful ones are usually those that concentrate on certain subjects and develop vertical and niche products. These startups mention the Invisible Web because they hope to appeal to users and investors by establishing that they are able to access this additional material. In other words, the Invisible Web represents added value. Well-established companies such as Deep Web Technologies and Bright Planet have been developing Invisible Web products for more than a decade now.

Competitive Intelligence is a research field for specialists in deep web searching. These practitioners usually offer a cross between business backgrounds and library science or research experience. They specialize in doing more than the general Google search that regular company staff members might be expected to perform for their businesses. They know how to gather information from many kinds of resources, and their research tool kits include Invisible Web resources and databases both free and proprietary. They work as consultants for corporations, and their product is their skill at sophisticated searching. Competitive Intelligence sites often mention the Invisible Web as part of the added value that they bring to their research product.

Search engine optimizers (SEOs) were mentioned previously for their part in altering search engine results. As businesses they bring a different perspective to the Invisible Web world. They are not interested in the Invisible Web as a research resource; rather, they want to help their clients emerge from the Invisible Web, or the little-used resources lost in long lists of search results. For them the Invisible Web is a no-man's-land to be avoided with their help.

SPECIALIZED RESEARCHERS

While not represented in the publication coverage included in Science-Direct, there is a world of specialized researchers—genealogists, medical researchers, archivists, and the like—interested in and working with the Invisible Web. Their objective is to find the most complete information possible, and they accomplish this by using all the tools available to them.

SUMMARY

It might be helpful at this point to summarize the various aspects of the Invisible Web discussed so far:

- The Invisible Web is a collection of diverse information resources.
- The Invisible Web is created because of the way in which general-purpose search engines are designed and function. As technology continues to develop, the content of the Invisible Web changes, but it continues to exist.

- Many Invisible Web resources reside in subscription databases or behind membership requirements. The fee-based web can be considered as part of the Invisible Web.
- The Invisible Web may also be created, in part, by the lack of knowledge about how to search for information.
- The Invisible Web is not easy to search.
- The Invisible Web's size is considerable but difficult to quantify. It represents many more resources than the surface web mined by general-purpose search engines.
- Those who are working with the Invisible Web and who are most interested in it tend to be in specialized fields.
- The Invisible Web is not commonly known or understood.

The final observation is both a fact and a question. If most people do not know about the existence of the Invisible Web, yet it is considered to hold valuable resources, then why is it not taught more widely?

In the chapters that follow, we will explore more about the ways research is being conducted and how it may be possible to teach the Invisible Web.

REFERENCES

Ankeny, Jason. 2010. "Gartner Forecasts Mobile Web Access Will Surpass PCs by 2013." *FierceMobileContent*, January 13. www.fiercemobilecontent.com/story/gartner-forecasts-mobile-web-access-will-surpass-pcs-2013/2010-01-13.

Badke, William. 2011. *Research Strategies: Finding Your Way through the Information Fog.* 4th ed. Lincoln, NE: iUniverse.com/Writers Club.

Bergman, Michael K. 2001. "The Deep Web: Surfacing Hidden Value." Bright-Planet white paper, September 24. http://brightplanet.com/wp-content/uploads/2012/03/12550176481-deepwebwhitepaper1.pdf.

Boswell, Wendy. 2007. *The About.com Guide to Online Research: Navigate the Web—from RSS and the Invisible Web to Multimedia and the Blogosphere.* About.com Guides. Avon, MA: Adams Media.

Cohen, Laura. 2013. "The Deep Web." *Internet Tutorials: Your Basic Guide to the Internet.* http://web.archive.org/web/201300602015752/http://internettutorials.net/deepweb.asp.

Devine, Jane, and Francine Egger-Sider. 2009. *Going Beyond Google: The Invisible Web in Learning and Teaching.* New York: Neal-Schuman.

Diaz, Karen. 2000. "The Invisible Web: Navigating the Web outside Traditional Search Engines." *Reference & User Services Quarterly* 40, no. 2: 131–134. Library Literature & Information Science Full Text.

Dogpile.com. 2007. "Different Engines, Different Results: Web Searchers Not Always Finding What They're Looking for Online." In collaboration with researchers from the Queensland University and the Pennsylvania State University. www.infospaceinc.com/files/Overlap-DifferentEnginesDifferent Results.pdf.

Ford, Nigel, and Yazdan Mansourian. 2006. "The Invisible Web: An Empirical Study of 'Cognitive Invisibility.'" *Journal of Documentation* 62, no. 5: 584–596. http://dx.doi.org/10.1108/00220410610688732.

Gil, Paul. 2012. "What Is the 'Invisible Web'?: The Content That Goes Beyond Google, Yahoo, Bing, and Ask.com." *Internet for Beginners*, About.com. http://netforbeginners.about.com/cs/secondaryweb1/a/secondaryweb.htm.

He, Bin, Mitesh Patel, Zhen Zhang, and Kevin Chen-Chuan Chang. 2007. "Accessing the Deep Web: A Survey." *Communications of the ACM* 50, no. 5: 94–101. http://dx.doi.org/10.1145/1230819.1241670.

Lewandowski, Dirk, and Philipp Mayr. 2006. "Exploring the Academic Invisible Web." *Library Hi Tech* 24, no. 4: 529–539. http://dx.doi.org/10.1108/07378830610715392.

Lovink, Geert. 2009. "Society of the Query: The Googlization of Our Lives." In *Deep Search: The Politics of Search Beyond Google*, edited by Konrad Becker and Felix Stalder, 45–53. Innsbruck: StudienVerlag.

Lyman, Peter, and Hal R. Varian. 2003. "How Much Information? 2003." School of Information Management and Systems, University of California at Berkeley. www2.sims.berkeley.edu/research/projects/how-much-info-2003/.

Madhavan, Jayant, David Ko, Łucja Kot, Vignesh Ganapathy, Alex Rasmussen, and Alon Halevy. 2008. "Google's Deep-Web Crawl." Paper presented at the 34th International Conference on Very Large Data Bases, VLDB '08, Auckland, New Zealand, August 23–28. www.vldb.org/pvldb/1/1454163.pdf.

Mui, Ylan Q., and Peter Whoriskey. 2010. "Facebook Passes Google as Most Popular Site on the Internet, Two Measures Show." *Washington Post*, December 31. www.washingtonpost.com/wp-dyn/content/article/2010/12/30/AR2010123004645.html.

O'Leary, Mick. 2010. "Hakia Gets Serious with Semantic Search." *Information Today* 27, no. 6: 38–40. Library, Information Science & Technology Abstracts with Full Text.

Siegel, David. 2009. *Pull: The Power of the Semantic Web to Transform Your Business*. New York: Portfolio.

Spencer, Brett. 2007. "Harnessing the Deep Web: A Practical Plan for Locating Free Specialty Databases on the Web." *Reference Services Review* 35, no. 1: 71–83. http://dx.doi.org/10.1108/00907320710729364.

"The Ultimate Guide to the Invisible Web." 2006. Online Education Database. http://oedb.org/library/college=basics/invisible-web.

Valenza, Joyce. 2009. "The New Invisible Web: On Searching Wikis and Tweets and Blogs and More." *NeverEndingSearch* (blog). *School Library Journal*, May 4. http://blog.schoollibraryjournal.com/neverendingsearch/2009/05/04/the-new-invisible-web-on-searching-wikis-and-tweets-and-blogs-and-more/.

Wouters, Paul, Colin Reddy, and Isidro Aguillo. 2006. "On the Visibility of Information on the Web: An Exploratory Experimental Approach." *Research Evaluation* 15, no. 2: 107–115. Academic Search Complete.

Zillman, Marcus. 2013. "Deep Web Research and Discovery Resources 2013." Virtual Private Library, July 1. www.deepwebresearch.info.

STUDIES OF
INFORMATION-SEEKING
BEHAVIOR

THE PREDECESSOR TO THIS BOOK, *GOING BEYOND Google*, included a thorough analysis of the use of the web for research which this chapter will update. Are students still primarily starting and ending research with Google, ignoring or simply bypassing the information sources their colleges offer? Have the advances in information technology made the Invisible Web more transparent, thus less invisible? This chapter will analyze studies of student information-seeking behavior, both nationwide and at single institutions, published since 2008. With the fast pace of technological advancement in the hardware and software used by students, what is the impact, if any, on how students proceed with research? The introduction of smartphones and tablet computers has changed not only how students access information, but, more importantly, what content they tap into. Faculty and librarians are experimenting with social networking sites, so prevalent in students' everyday lives. But the more important question remains how these social networking and social media sites can be harnessed for research purposes. The literature needs to catch up with use. It seems, so far, that the greatest use of the latest technology is for everyday life needs rather than academic research.

Who are the students whose information-seeking behavior we wish to understand? The youngest, those born after 1993, have been nicknamed the "Google Generation" (Nicholas et al. 2011, 29); "digital natives" refer to those born in the Internet age and raised with the Internet (Prensky 2001, 1); "Millennials," born after 1980, were "the first generation to come of age in the new millennium" (Taylor and Keeter 2010, 4); "Generation Y" refers to those born between 1973 and 1994 (Nicholas et al. 2011, 29); and the "Net Generation" (Tapscott 2008) refers to those born after 1985. Their study habits can increasingly be reduced to two imperatives: connectedness and ease of use. How, if at all, do the characteristics of these digital natives affect their research skills? The first part of this chapter will look at the convenience factor, analyzing studies of information-seeking behavior, while the second part will deal with personalization and connectedness, the latter affected by the ever-growing use of mobile technology.

In *Going Beyond Google*, published in 2009, the latest study reviewed had been issued in 2008. Review of the literature since 2008 does not, at first glance, indicate that much has changed in students' information-seeking behavior. "I just Google it" seems to be the leitmotiv for students conducting research, whether for academic purposes or for everyday life problems. The use of the web is so pervasive that, by 2006, *Google* had become a verb in the English language (*Merriam-Webster*), with derivatives such as *Googling, Googleized* or *Googlized*, and *Googlization*, and, as we have seen, an entire generation has been named after the search engine. There continues to be a proliferation of studies, large and small, scrutinizing students' information-seeking behavior in the hope of providing services—in our case, library services—better suited to the Google Generation. A large percentage of the studies undertaken in the past four years point to the same types of information-seeking behavior as earlier studies, the overarching finding being that students, for the most part, start their searches for a research paper with Google and ignore library databases, where the bulk of the Invisible Web resides. The factors pinpointed earlier for the popularity of general-purpose search engines were ease of use, convenience, time savings, availability of full text, and timeliness of resources. But the problems associated with relying on general-purpose search engines exclusively continue to plague today's student: retrieval limits, search strategy problems, and evaluation issues (Devine and Egger-Sider 2009, 28–31). This chapter will highlight a wide range of studies before delving into the impact of new technologies on how today's students search for information.

OVERVIEW STUDIES

Among the many user behavior or information-seeking behavior studies published since 2008, three stand out, though each presents an overview of previously published work. Nonetheless, with their global perspective, these three studies provide a fresh look at user behavior. The first one is *The Digital Information Seeker: Report of the Findings from Selected OCLC, RIN, and JISC User Behaviour Projects* (Connaway and Dickey 2010), issued on behalf of the Joint Information Systems Committee (JISC), "the UK's expert on information and digital technologies for education and research" (www.jisc. ac.uk). This report reviews twelve studies undertaken from 2005 to 2009,[1] some of which were analyzed in our earlier book. However, they all merit a second glance: the report traces user behavior by trait, showing how each study addresses that trait. The most salient of these traits are the "centrality of Google" in searching; the use of keywords to access content, including e-journal content; the overwhelming emphasis on speed and convenience; a tendency to review only a few pages of results; and a habit of "'bouncing' between resources" (Connaway and Dickey 2010, 34). This complement of behaviors privileges free, visible web content over the riches of the Invisible Web, the latter of which is primarily located in databases available through libraries. The report ends with a recommendation that libraries strengthen their offerings of digitized content to meet students' needs and expectations—in other words, ironically, to make the library more like Google.

A more recent article, by Connaway, Dickey, and Radford (2011), analyzes two reports, both multiyear studies funded by the Institute of Museum and Library Services. These reports, *Sense-Making the Information Confluence* and *Seeking Synchronicity*, discussed also in the JISC report noted above, here receive greater emphasis on the concept of convenience linked to the theory of *satisficing* (*satisfying* + *sufficing*), the latter an extension of rational choice theory. According to the article, "Convenience includes the choice of the information source (is it readily accessible online or in print), the satisfaction with the source (does it contain the needed information and is it easy to use), and the time it will take to access and use the information source" (188). Students find information that is "good enough": they pull up results quickly through Google and use the ones they find "convenient" without fully evaluating their sources.

Another overview study is a Centre for Information Behaviour and the Evaluation of Research (CIBER) report, also published on behalf of JISC: *Scholarly Digital Use and Information-Seeking Behaviour in Business and Economics* (Nicholas et al. 2010). It reviews four studies, all of which formed part of CIBER's Virtual Scholar research program:

- *JISC National E-books Observatory* (NEBO) (2007–2009)
- *RIN E-journal Study* (2007)
- *Elsevier Authors as Users Study* (2003–2005)
- *MaxData Study* (2005–2006)

Analysis of log entries by tens of thousands of business and economics students in the United Kingdom showed that

> Business/Economics students and academic staff use and seek information very much like their virtual colleagues in other subject fields. That is they make characteristically short visits, which see only a few pages and documents viewed; they like simple searching, use Google and Google Scholar and like browsing when they get to a website; they appreciate searching off-site and outside the traditional (9–5) working day (Nicholas et al. 2010, 6).

NATIONAL STUDIES

With very few exceptions, the larger studies published in England and in the United States since 2008 come to the same conclusions about the major information-seeking traits of students doing research, with convenience and ease of access being the primary motivators. Access trumps content in most cases: users will sacrifice content for convenience.

The ECAR [EDUCAUSE Center for Applied Research] Study of Undergraduate Students and Information Technology, conducted annually since 2004, reports for 2010 on a web-based survey of students at 100 colleges and universities in the United States and 27 community colleges in the United States and Canada (Smith and Caruso 2010). Regarding information literacy skills,

81% of students surveyed "considered themselves expert or very skilled in searching the Internet effectively and efficiently," and 57% "rated their ability to evaluate the reliability and credibility of online information as expert or very skilled" (9). In addition, 94% of students reported using their school's library website "for school, work, or recreation" (10). While self-rating may not accurately reflect student abilities, the self-reported tendency to use library resources (and hence Invisible Web resources) seems strong.

The OCLC study *Perceptions of Libraries, 2010: Context and Community* (De Rosa et al. 2010) analyzes the library as a "brand" and compares the 2010 data to the data in its previous report (2005). OCLC compiled statistics about library users in general and by age group. College students represented 19% of the survey participants. Overall, 92% of the general population surveyed used Google or another search engine, 73% used Wikipedia, and 33% the library website (De Rosa et al. 2010, 42, 33); of this same population, 84% *started* their searches with a search engine, 3% started with Wikipedia, and none started with a library website (32–33). The percentages for college students are roughly comparable: when searching online, 93% used a search engine, 88% used Wikipedia, and 57% use a library website (52). While students overwhelmingly value "speed, convenience, reliability and ease of use" (54), it is interesting that the percentage of college students who *start* research with a search engine (83%) is down from the percentage in 2005 (92%). Similar to the general population, college students do not initiate research on a library website, 1% start with online databases, and 7% start with Wikipedia (54). On the other hand, 27% of college students who start their research with a general-purpose search engine end up on a library website (57). Overall, "results show a decline in use of library Web sites, electronic journals and online databases since 2005" (52)—that is, a decline in the use of Invisible Web content. In general, "students are less impressed with all online resources" than they had been in 2005 (59). Could this change be correlated to the fact that students seem to rely more in 2010 on their own personal knowledge and "common sense," corroborated by social networking connections, to judge whether or not to use an information source? The use of social networking sites and social media, although not yet pervasive for college research, seems to have shifted the axis of authority from objective factors such as the CARS Checklist for Information Quality (Harris 2010) to personal recommendations gleaned from "friends." What this shift portends for reaching resources in the Invisible Web remains an unanswered question.

The studies above have shown that users prefer search engines, and in particular Google, which enjoys a two-thirds market share (comScore 2013), and resources such as Wikipedia that are part of the visible web, over the electronic resources provided by public or academic libraries, the bulk of which constitute the Invisible Web (see table 2.1). The next few studies come to the conclusion that researchers do not use visible web content exclusively, particularly in what is known as everyday life research, or ELR.

TABLE 2.1

Analysis of online searching behavior

Population	Use			Start with		
	Search engine	Library website	Wikipedia	Search engine	Library website	Wikipedia
General	92%	33%	73%	84%	0	3%
College students	93%	57%	88%	83%*	0	7%

* Down from 92% in 2005

Source: *Perceptions of Libraries, 2010* (OCLC)

Two studies by Alison J. Head and Michael B. Eisenberg, sponsored by Project Information Literacy (PIL), investigate the duality, also mentioned in the OCLC study (De Rosa et al. 2010), between student reliance on Google results and their use of articles from library subscription databases. In 2009, Head and Eisenberg discovered through an online survey of 2,318 students, at six colleges and universities in the United States, that students found information using Google for all types of research but that, for course-related research, many also used scholarly databases such as EBSCO, JSTOR, or ProQuest (Head and Eisenberg 2009, 1, 3). In general, students use an information-seeking strategy that is "close at hand, tried and true" (3). Students do not want to rock the boat; on the contrary, they want to stick to an information-seeking strategy that they are familiar with. They favor "brevity, consensus, and currency" (33). In 2010, in a much larger study, this time of 8,353 students at twenty-five U.S. colleges and universities, Head and Eisenberg came to essentially the same conclusions (2010a, 7).

In their article "How College Students Use the Web to Conduct Everyday Life Research" (2011), Head and Eisenberg use data from the 2010 PIL study, finding that the students' primary sources of information were almost exclusively free web content: search engines, including Google

(95%), friends and family (87%), Wikipedia (84%), classmates (81%), social networking sites (70%), and government sites (63%) (Head and Eisenberg 2011, fig. 2).

A British study of business and economics students and researchers at three universities came to a similar conclusion as the studies above: "Students and researchers from Business and Economics use both resources subscribed by the library and those freely available on the Internet when seeking information in the academic context" (Wong et al. 2009, 5). The authors note that the more advanced the academic level, the more the library databases are used. When researchers use freely available resources, the order of use is Google, Google Scholar, Wikipedia, and YouTube (5).

Two studies, one in the United States and one in the United Kingdom, uncovered some students who use databases as their *initial* research. The American study, by Niu et al. (2010), queried 2,063 academic researchers in science, medicine, and engineering at five universities across the country. Respondents' primary search tools were citation/bibliographic databases *followed by* general web search engines (Niu et al. 2010, 876–877). The British study, by Hampton-Reeves et al. (2009), surveyed 429 students at the University of Central Lancashire plus three other anonymous institutions in 2009. The survey showed that, for online research, 80% of students use the library catalog, more than they use Google or Google Scholar. Graduate students gravitated toward Google Scholar over Google, and favored peer-reviewed material: "Students value relevance and academic quality above everything else when identifying and using research" (33).

Several studies have reported on the general population as opposed to academic cohorts. As a follow-up to the 2007 JISC-funded report titled *Information Behaviour of the Researcher of the Future* (UCL 2008)[2] which analyzed the information-seeking behavior of the "Google Generation," the CIBER research group was approached by the BBC to film 80 persons from the general public conducting web searches on computer terminals at University College London (Nicholas et al. 2011). The research was to determine whether there are age-related differences in the web search behavior of the general public. One of the results was that "the Google Generation proved to be the quickest information searchers, spending the least amount of time on a question" (42), confirming what has been said all along: that this generation has "the propensity to rush, rely on point-and-click, first-up-on-Google answers, along with growing . . . inability to evaluate information, . . . too often sacrificing depth for breadth" (44). However, in spite of answering questions faster, with fewer clicks per question, using primarily natural language, members of the Google Generation were less confident about their answers (44). Having grown up with technology, they are extremely adept at obtaining results but less comfortable about the value of the results retrieved. The CIBER Google Generation Research Programme is looking further into understanding web behavior (UCL [2011]). This study points toward the need for information literacy education. It is one thing to search for and find information; it is quite another to be adept with the tools necessary to evaluate the results, and to choose sources appropriate to the question at hand. In the United States, the Pew Research Center study also shows the prevalence of search engine use among the general population: 92% of online adults use search engines to find information on the web, and the higher the education level, the more they use the Internet (Purcell 2011, 3).

Table 2.2 summarizes studies of more than one academic institution or across a general population, listed in ascending chronological order. Overview studies are not included. Table 2.3 summarizes studies limited to states or single institutions (covered in the next section). In each table, boldface codes have been assigned to correlate national studies with those in the tables of information-seeking behaviors (tables 2.4–2.6).

STATE AND SINGLE-INSTITUTION STUDIES

A group of academic libraries in Illinois and a number of single institutions have produced newer studies (table 2.3). *ERIAL (Ethnographic Research in Illinois Academic Libraries)* used ethnographic methods to discover how their students conduct research. Although the research method was new, the conclusions were similar to the national studies looked at above: overuse of Google and keyword searching, with librarians not on students' radar (Asher, Duke, and Green 2010).

A two-phase study at the University of Minnesota, *Discoverability* (Hanson et al. 2009; 2010), found several trends: students are using resources outside library systems, rely on keywords in Google, and seem content with "good enough" results; for University of Minnesota users, discovery (content) and delivery (access) weigh equally. Du and Evans (2011) interviewed

TABLE 2.2
National studies

Author of study / Code	Year	Location	Sample	Methodology
Hampton-Reeves et al. / **UCLan**	2009	University of Central Lancashire and three anonymous universities	429 students	Survey; focus groups; recordings of student searches; case studies
Head and Eisenberg / **PIL***	2009	Six colleges and universities in the U.S.	2,318 students	Online survey
Wong et al. / **JISC**	2009	Three universities in England	34 students in business and economics	Observation study plus in-depth interviews
De Rosa et al. / **OCLC**	2010	Canada, UK, and U.S.	2,229 library users ages fourteen and over	Online survey; subset of college students (19%)
Head and Eisenberg / **PIL**	2010	Twenty-five colleges and universities in the U.S.	8,353 college students	Online survey—data part of PIL Project
Niu et al. / **Niu**	2010	Five universities in the U.S.	2,063 academic researchers in science, medicine, and engineering	Web-based questionnaire
Smith and Caruso / **ECAR**	2010	100 four-year institutions in the U.S. and 27 U.S. and Canadian two-year schools	36,950 students	Web-based quantitative survey; student focus groups; student comments; longitudinal comparisons with previous surveys
Head and Eisenberg*	2011	Twenty-five campuses in the U.S.	8,353 college students	Online survey—data part of PIL Project
Nicholas et al., CIBER** / **Nicholas**	2011	University College London (UCL) Science Library	80 people at UCL and 58 in remote locations	Filmed library patrons searching on public terminals**
Purcell, Pew Internet & American Life Project / **Purcell**	2011		2,227 adults ages eighteen and over	Phone survey in English and Spanish

*The 2010 PIL study by Head and Eisenberg includes data from the 2009 study for comparison. The article in *First Monday* (2011) is a recap of the data in the 2010 report. So only the 2010 report is included in tables 2.4–2.6.

**The BBC/CIBER study undertaken at the UCL Science Library filmed anyone who volunteered from the public who volunteered. So this study is of the general public at large, rather than an academic cohort.

TABLE 2.3

State and single-institution studies

Author of study / Code	Year	Location	Sample	Methodology
Asher, Duke, and Green / **ERIAL** (**Ethnographic Research in Illinois Academic Libraries**)	2010	Five campuses in Illinois	161 students, 75 faculty, and 48 librarians	Two anthropologists with faculty and librarians on each campus collected data through open-ended interviews and direct observations
Dubicki / **Dubicki**	2010	Monmouth University Business School	39 students (54% seniors) plus 298 usable surveys	Survey; qualitative and quantitative phases
Hanson et al. / **Discover**	2009–2010	University of Minnesota	University of Minnesota library website users	Analysis of trends from user studies and statistics for local discovery systems; conducted in two phases: (1) data gathering and (2) strategies for the future
Hargittai et al. / **Hargittai**	2010	Large, urban public research institution	102 first-year students	Observations and interviews
Du and Evans / **Du**	2011	QUT Brisbane, Australia	11 PhD students (subsample of study of 42 postgraduates)	Observation of online research behavior
Judd and Kennedy / **Judd**	2011	University in Australia	842 first- through third-year medical students	Detailed logs of Internet usage in labs
Kingsley et al. / **Kingsley**	2011	University of Nevada, Las Vegas	160 first-year dental students	Assignment followed by survey

eleven PhD students at Queensland University of Technology in Brisbane, Australia, and found that 64% used Google as a starting point and 18% Google Scholar, because both were easier to use than library databases. They stuck largely to basic search functions. However, 91% did use multiple searches in Google products as well as in library databases.

Studies in different disciplines seem to point in the same direction. An Australian study of medical students showed that "Google and Wikipedia were the most frequently used sites despite students rating them as the least reliable of the five sites investigated. The library . . . was the least used site" (Judd and Kennedy 2011, 351). Students further along in their studies tended to "rely on more authoritative sources and combine their use of Google and Wikipedia with these sources" (355). Similar conclusions were reached by Kingsley et al. (2011) in their look at first-year dental students at the University of Nevada at Las Vegas. Google was the first port of call, followed by PubMed, Wikipedia, and Google Scholar (1, 3–5). These two studies stress that even for evidence-based research, medical students turn to Google and Wikipedia. In other words, medical students are not tapping into Invisible Web content for their research, at least initially. Another study found that business students at Monmouth University rarely used books; moreover, 47% started their research in Google, 27% through the library's website. Many students did use library databases but had trouble navigating them (Dubicki 2010).

In yet another study with first-year students in an urban, public university (Hargittai et al. 2010), the authors concluded that students often trust the first search result because they have faith in the relevancy ranking of the search engine they identify and, therefore, do not feel the need to evaluate the source itself any further. Just as in the OCLC study mentioned above (De Rosa et al. 2010), students tended to identify with a particular search engine (Google, followed by Yahoo), and that association gave them the confidence that the information retrieved was credible. Furthermore, considerable variations in skill levels were observed when it came to evaluation of sources (Hargittai et al. 2010). As Head and Eisenberg (2011) noted in their article on everyday life research, motivation plays a crucial part in how far students will pursue a search and assess the relevance of the search results.

In summary, the studies looked at in this chapter highlight a certain number of recurring traits. The major ones are an over-reliance on Google and other major search engines, a tendency to favor time over content, and an overwhelming preference for convenience. Tables 2.4 through 2.6 attempt to codify today's students' major information-seeking behaviors. Students who use Invisible Web content remain in the minority.

THE NARROWING OF THE INVISIBLE WEB

Many technological changes have taken place in the last three years that are changing the definition of the Invisible Web and have a direct bearing on how students today conduct research. Advances in Google, the general-purpose search engine most used by the majority of users, including students, have narrowed the Invisible Web: as Google crawlers pick up and index more and more data, it becomes visible and, in many cases, freely available. The first chapter of this book dealt with some of these changes; studies of the impact of Google Scholar and Google Books are discussed below.

GOOGLE SCHOLAR

Google Scholar "provides a search of scholarly literature across many disciplines and sources, including theses, books, abstracts and articles" (http://scholar.google.com). In a recent study of Google Scholar, Xiaotian Chen (2010) found a "dramatic" improvement in Google Scholar coverage of academic journal articles from vendors who partner with it. Not only is more and more data available through Google Scholar, but most colleges today make use of the ability to link their subscription databases to it, providing their students with full-text access to articles. This type of enabling takes advantage of students' behavior patterns by allowing them to use their preferred search engine while also offering them full-text access to articles within vetted databases. Google Scholar, as a result, uncovers Invisible Web material to students through a familiar search engine.

The danger, however, is that students will come to rely on Google Scholar entirely. There is a large body of literature on Google Scholar that analyzes its attributes, both positive and negative. Most students do not know how Google Scholar functions nor what it covers. Péter Jacsó, who has written many articles on Google Scholar, warns that "GS undoubtedly has the broadest source base, but it is still the most enigmatic database. It does not provide any details about the sources it uses, the number of records collected, the number of journals, conference proceedings, conference papers, books, book series, Masters' theses, doctoral dissertations, bibliographies,

TABLE 2.4
Behaviors associated with visible web searching

Study	Start with a search engine	Overuse Google	Use Google suite	Access e-journals through Google	Use Wikipedia	Believe search engines are easier to use	Don't stay long on one page	Use keywords only
JISC 2009	Use Google and Google Scholar				Third choice			
UCLan 2009	23.5%	✓	Google Schclar	✓				✓
Discover 2010		✓	✓	✓				✓
Dubicki 2010	46.6%; 14% textbooks				5.7% to start; 40% never used it			
ERIAL 2010		✓						
Hargittai 2010	✓	✓			35%			
OCLC 2010	93% for college students	Two-thirds of searches		14%	88%	83%		
PIL 2010	96% used course readings; 92% Google				84% for everyday life research; 73% for course work	✓		
Du 2011	64% with Google; 18% with Google Scholar		Google Schclar	✓		✓		
Judd 2011	70%	✓			51%	✓		
Kingsley 2011	42.5%; 8% Google Scholar	✓			17%			
Nicholas 2011							Yes for Google Generation	
Purcell 2011	92% of online adults							

Note: Studies for which there is no data under these categories were not included in this table.

TABLE 2.5

Why users like/dislike using the visible web

Study	Ease-of-use	Convenience	Time is of the essence	Consider themselves expert at searching	Perceive themselves as good at evaluation	Too much info	Consider results "good enough"
JISC 2009			✓				
UCLan 2009		✓			Relevance is key; look to external validation	✓	
Discover 2010	✓	✓					✓
Dubicki 2010	✓						
ECAR 2010		✓		81%	57%		
OCLC 2010	✓	90%	✓	✓			
PIL 2010		✓		✓		✓	
Du 2011	✓						
Judd 2011	✓	✓	✓				
Kingsley 2011					No		
Nicholas 2011			✓	No for Google Generation	No		

Note: Studies for which there is no data under these categories were not included in this table.

TABLE 2.6

Behaviors associated with Invisible Web searching

Study	Start in a database	Find databases confusing	Librarians not on students' radar	Trust that websites are reliable	Rely heavily on friends and family	Ask an expert	Library website
JISC 2009	✓	✓		✓	✓		✓
UClan 2009	18% start in database			Must be relevant to assignment			32% start with lib catalog; 80% use it at some point
Discover 2010				✓			
Dubicki 2010	✓	Database users had more problems than Google users	28% consulted them		24%		27%
ECAR 2010							94%
ERIAL 2010		✓	✓				
Niu 2010	✓						✓
OCLC 2010	30%			43%		136% in-crease since 2005	58%
PIL 2010	Use databases		30%; 14% for everyday life research	56% relied on web-site design; 54% on familiarity	61%		
Du 2011	18%		✓				
Hargittai 2010				✓ (trust brands)	19%		
Judd 2011							13%
Kingsley 2011	32%						

Note: Studies for which there is no data under these categories were not included in this table.

patents, court opinions, and PowerPoint files of presentations and their subject coverage. Neither is there any indication of the timeframe of its coverage" (2011, 157). On the other hand, Google Scholar is a treasure trove of information, the best part, for students, being the links to full-text articles from databases owned by their respective colleges and universities. A study by Dirk Lewandowski, who has written about the "Academic Invisible Web," shows that for journal articles in library and information science, Google Scholar "can be used in many cases to easily find available full texts of articles already identified using another tool" (Lewandowski 2010, 250). William Walters claims that "in terms of both recall and precision, Google Scholar performs better than most of the subscription databases" (2009, 5). Given the fact that Google Scholar is a familiar brand to students because of their reliance on its sister search engine for the majority of their searches, whether for academic research or everyday life research, it behooves faculty to introduce Google Scholar as part of a discussion on research, and in spite of any ongoing limitations. The studies outlined earlier in this chapter show a difference in search behavior as the level of education increases (Connaway and Dickey 2010; Du and Evans 2011; Hampton-Reeves et al. 2009; Judd and Kennedy 2011; Nicholas et al. 2010; Wong et al. 2009). Graduate students do make greater use of Google Scholar and use it as a stepping stone to delve further into Invisible Web territory such as the library catalog and the specialized databases offered by their institution of higher learning.

GOOGLE BOOKS

Google Books originated in 2004 with an agreement between Google and five research libraries to digitize their print collections. The questions for this study are whether Google Books reduces the Invisible Web footprint and how students and faculty are using Google Books in their research. Google Books opens up a huge territory that was previous invisible. For a large number of books which are still under copyright, Google Books offers only snippets or a limited preview. Students are known to use that preview as a source for research papers. However, what they see can be such a narrow view of the entire book that they could be misled as to its overall argument.

In a brilliantly perceptive column entitled "The Great Research Disaster" (2009), William Badke depicts the research pitfalls of a student who picks at previews in Google Books, wanders around Google Scholar without understanding what he is looking at, and remains oblivious to the riches of library databases and librarians' services. Badke gets at the essence of the research disaster by showing that, in the end, this student worked hard at putting this paper together, searching more than one website, remembering enough to look for books and articles, perusing the references at the end of the article in Wikipedia—yet without ever really grasping what research is all about. Too many resources were invisible, and the library represented a brand that had no familiarity, no ease of access.

PERSONALIZATION

A new concern has been brought to the surface in a very vivid manner by Eli Pariser in his recent book, *The Filter Bubble*. Search engines, in their attempt to personalize the search experience of their users, largely for commercial reasons, are narrowing the information web that users start with, based on their previous clicks. Hence, two people sitting side by side at two computers and executing exactly the same search using Google will obtain different results. Google instituted personalized search for everyone in 2009 (Horling and Kulick 2009). This new direction, Pariser argues, poses serious threats to the freedom of information access and is creating information silos into which users are unknowingly placed. This situation adds a new meaning to the phrase Invisible Web. The user who executes a search about a political party will not see an objective, diversified array of sources about that party. And, more detrimental, from then on, the search engine will steer that user toward information within the worldview of someone from that party. Completely unaware, the user is now stuck in an information "bubble" of Google's making. Pariser summarizes: "Like a lens, the filter bubble invisibly transforms the world we experience by controlling what we see and don't see" (Pariser 2011, 82). This personalization of the web poses a new minefield for students who, like most web users, have no clue that a so-called general-purpose search engine has them enveloped in an information bubble, clouding their ability to conduct an objective search. Pariser takes this idea a step further when he argues that this information bubble will affect how our brains function: "But the rise of the filter bubble doesn't just affect how we process news. It can also affect how we think" (76), and the danger is that "a perfectly filtered world would provoke less learning" (91).

In a contribution to the edited volume *Deep Search: The Politics of Search Beyond Google*, Stalder and Mayer discuss, in a chapter titled "The Second Index: Search Engines, Personalization and Surveillance," how Google gathers data on users and divides the data into three areas:

- "the knowledge person"—what the user clicks on;
- "the social person"—whom the user connects with via e-mail or social networks; and
- "the embodied person"—where the user is physically located (Stalder and Mayer 2009, 112)

Google obtains these data through interaction, "click tracking," logs, cookies (100–101), as well as "collaborative filtering" (Feuz, Fuller, and Stalder 2011). How do these new relevancy-focused search results affect students' research? To suggest one example, if a history professor's requirement is a research paper on the rise of the Tea Party in American politics, each student will pull up a different results list even when using similar keywords. The students' previous online histories, what they have clicked on in the past, where they are physically located, and with whom they have been in contact will drive the results that Google returns. The more it knows about us, the more the search engine will present us with information and ideas that already conform to our individual mindset, thereby simply reinforcing beliefs held and not exposing us to new or contradictory ideas and points of views from which to learn. Searching in an information bubble impedes learning.

Also disconcerting is the fact that most students are not aware of the existence of these "filter bubbles" even as they manipulate their personal online information silos. A person is the sum of various attributes depending on the context: one's work personality could be very different from one's personality at home. For the most part, students and researchers in general never realize that search engines keep some information from them, let alone specifically which sites are effectively invisible to them. The entire concept of personalization is "subtly pushing users to see the world according to criteria pre-defined by Google" (Feuz, Fuller, and Stalder 2011). Google is proceeding in this direction not to help users find more relevant results but to give advertisers more targeted users. The implications for the majority of students—who begin and end their research using Google—are staggering: students will never be presented with a full picture of a topic because their search results will more and more be filtered through what machines have decided constitutes "who they are." In *The Googlization of Everything*, Siva Vaidhyanathan says: "Learning is by definition an encounter with what you don't know, what you haven't thought of, what you couldn't conceive, and what you never understood or entertained as possible. It's an encounter with the other—even with otherness as such. . . . The kind of filter that

Google interposes between an Internet searcher and what a search yields shields the searcher from radical encounters with the other by 'personalizing' the results" (Vaidhyanathan 2011, 182).

SOCIAL NETWORKING SITES

Another new development that muddies the landscape of the Invisible Web is the growth of social networking sites (SNS) and their impact on students' information-seeking behavior. According to a Pew Research Center report, "The number of those using social networking sites has nearly doubled since 2008 and the population of SNS users has gotten older" (Hampton et al. 2011, 3). Social networking sites are used primarily for keeping up with friends and sharing content but use up 23% of time spent online (Nielsen 2011, 2).

There is not yet a great deal of research analyzing how social media are used by students and researchers and what impact they have on their information-seeking behavior. The 2010 ECAR study cited earlier shows that only 3 out of 10 students use social networking sites in their courses, half use them to "communicate with classmates about course-related topics, but fewer than 1 in 10 (8%) said they use them to communicate with instructors about course-related topics" (Smith and Caruso 2010, 14). The CIBER research group at University College London (UCL) has just published two similar articles analyzing the results of close to 2,000 online surveys sent to researchers, editors, administrators, and librarians worldwide on the use of social media in research: "Social Media Use in the Research Workflow" appeared in *Learned Publishing* (Rowlands et al. 2011) and in *Information Services & Use* (Nicholas and Rowlands 2011). The study broke social media into eight categories: social networking (Facebook and Linked In), blogging (WordPress and Blogger), microblogging (Twitter), collaborative authoring tools (Google Docs), social tagging and bookmarking (Delicious and CiteULike), scheduling and meeting tools (Doodle), conferencing (Skype), and image or video sharing (YouTube, SlideShare, and Flickr). It is apparent that researchers prefer known, established social tools, which the authors call "household brands," rather than specialized tools for their subject expertise (Nicholas and Rowlands 2011, 82). The three most popular activities are working collaboratively (62.7% of respondents), through a software such as Google Docs, followed by conferencing (48.3%), through tools such as Skype, and using scheduling and meeting tools (41%) such as Doodle. See figure 2.1. There are variations in use among disciplines and age.

FIGURE 2.1 **Popularity of various types of social media**

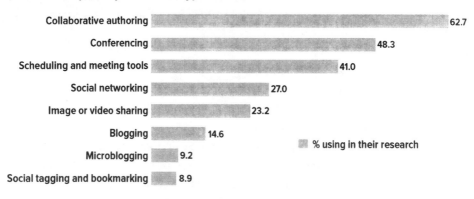

Source: "Social Media Use in the Research Workflow" (Nicholas and Rowlands 2011, 63).

Whereas, according to the CIBER study, "social networking is most useful for the dissemination of research findings, in research collaboration, and, perhaps surprisingly, in helping to identify research opportunities" (Rowlands et al. 2011, 190), it is still not clear what the role of social media is in the actual research process. The only difference between users of social media and the smaller control group, members of which had never used social media in research, was "that the active, social media-aware researcher [was] much more likely to put out a general call for information, perhaps on a listserv or a social network" (Rowlands et al. 2011, 192). This study seems to indicate that, at this time, social media are used primarily in scholarly communication and in the dissemination of research rather than in the actual search process itself. The data show that, whether researchers are users of social media or not, they conduct research on the free web as the first port of call followed by "licensed e-content made available through their institutional library" (Rowlands et al. 2011, 192). Organizations such as the Social Science Research Network facilitate the distribution and dissemination of scholarly literature but operate in a hybrid manner: searching and viewing is part of the surface web, whereas submitting a paper or subscribing to an e-journal resides in the Invisible Web. There are a growing number of such networks, academic as well as professional: Sermo for physicians; SurroundHealth for health professionals; edWeb.net for the education community; art-humanities.net, based in the UK but open to anyone, for research and teaching in the digital arts and humanities;

myExperiment, also based in the UK, for scientists. These organizations provide their members with resources, best practices, and the ability to communicate and share with one another, a new and growing segment of the Invisible Web.

Some faculty are incorporating one type or another of social media, particularly Twitter, within their teaching, and there is a growing body of literature describing this phenomenon (Jacobsen and Forste 2011; Silver 2011; Young 2009). David Silver, professor of media studies and environmental studies at the University of San Francisco, explains that he uses Twitter because the accounts are public and, as such, they make students "become ... more responsible for their work," and because it "simplifies course management" (Silver 2011, B34). But, according to this body of literature, tweets are primarily used to discuss or comment within a class. The information shared seems to be of limited use to students doing research at the present time, but it may grow in importance over the years.

The social networking sites used within an individual class are usually password-protected, especially if used in conjunction with course management software, which has its own level of security. The site, then, can be used only by the students enrolled in that particular class, making it invisible to anyone outside of that bubble, to use Eli Pariser's terminology. This scenario does not offer research possibilities for other students to stumble upon on their own. A discussion on Facebook, for example in an English class working on Mark Twain, will not be picked up by other college students who might also be writing a paper on Mark Twain. Stephen Arnold calls Facebook the "walled garden," because the information is regulated by privacy settings and typically made available only to "friends." He suggests that, "by definition, the content indexed and the pages identified within the Facebook walled garden, which is open to members only, is more subjective than ordinary web search" (Arnold 2010, 20).

Even though information within the walled garden is available only to its members, students could use that private interface to conduct research. How would that research be undertaken? Friends could recommend websites, articles, or books to each other within that space. Someone could also post a question on his or her wall: Has anyone ever done research on Mark Twain? Can you recommend sources for a research paper? The title of Stephen Arnold's article in *Information Today* is very apt: "Is a Search Revolution Brewing?" This type of search within social networking sites is reminiscent of vertical or niche searching in that it searches within a specific subject for a specific audience. The difference is that a human element has been brought back into the equation: recommendations from friends.

Research has shown that Wikipedia, the collaboratively generated compendium of knowledge, is heavily used by students, primarily for background information (Head and Eisenberg 2010b). Very much part of the visible web, Wikipedia is often the first result in a Google search. Kim, Yoo-Lee, and Sin note that Wikipedia is heavily used for background or introduction to a topic as well as for everyday life information (80%), followed by YouTube (69%) and Q&A sites (60%); on the other hand, social networking sites such as Facebook and Twitter are still used primarily for everyday life situations (Kim, Yoo-Lee, and Sin 2011, 2). Stuart Hampton-Reeves, in his study of college students in England, predicts that "one area in which social networks might have a beneficial effect is in the translation and energizing of existing informal networks which students may already use to identify research content" (2009, 11).

Social bookmarking enables the storing and sharing of recommended or favorite websites. There is a myriad of such sites: Pinterest, Delicious, StumbleUpon, Diigo, Digg, Reddit, and Newsvine for news, Flickr for pictures, Technorati for blogs, CiteULike for academics; the list is unlimited. There is a fine line between what is visible and invisible within these social bookmarking sites. Depending on the site, the user may be able to log in and regulate privacy settings. Users "tag" their saved sites to facilitate recall and organization within similar subjects. Of course, the goal is not only to collect bookmarked sites but to share them with others. But, in our context, the question that begs to be asked is: Are these bookmarking sites used in research? In "Social Search: A Taxonomy of, and a User-Centred Approach to, Social Web Search," the coauthors, both of the School of Library and Information Studies at the University of Alberta in Canada, suggest that "social bookmarking tags could help users form better queries" (McDonnell and Shiri 2011, 16). They go on to describe four cases in which searches were enhanced with the help of Delicious. After an initial Google search, a particular URL look-up was performed in Delicious; this led the user to examine the tags that other people had used in conjunction with that particular site as well as to follow those people who had bookmarked it. This method, the article presents, could lead users to follow experts in particular domains and discover new vocabulary for approaching a certain topic.

The Google search will unearth sources in the visible web while a search in Delicious might lead the user to tagged sources from the Invisible Web.

MOBILE DEVICES AND APPS

According to the latest Nielsen *Social Media Report* published in December 2012, "[m]ore people are using smartphones and tablets to access social media. . . . Forty-six percent of social media users say they use their smartphone to access social media; 16 percent say they connect to social media using a tablet" (Nielsen 2012). The runaway use of mobile devices and tablet computers has created a new information silo: "apps," or applications that can be downloaded onto a smartphone from a website. According to Harry McCracken, blogger for Technologizer, Apple and Google each claim, in 2013, the availability of more than 800,000 apps for their respective platforms, iOS and Android (McCracken 2013). Nielsen, however, reports that most people spend their time only with the top fifty apps (Nielsen 2011). Apps give direct access to a field of information, such as weather, e-books, restaurant reviews, Facebook, etc., without the necessity of doing a web search. Apps resemble vertical searching in that they do not search across a horizontal expanse as does Google but drill down within a particular subject. In one of the first cross-institution analyses of how the mobile Web is used for academic purposes, Alan Aldrich writes: "Smartphone users could accomplish most tasks using the full web, but an app condenses information into prepackaged forms. Mobile web users access a different app for each function or information need, with each app being a discrete unit isolated from the larger context" (Aldrich 2010, [2]). As the figure 2.2 demonstrates, apps are being used primarily for everyday situations, with games, weather, social networking, and maps the most downloaded onto smartphones.

There are also a number of educational apps available for smartphones and tablets. What is their impact on students' research behavior other than providing instant access to the Internet? The information is provided in a different medium but only presentation, not content, is affected. Science textbooks available in e-book format are downloadable onto smartphones or tablets. Apps still lag in technology, however, when it comes to elaborate scientific or medical illustrations, which may not fit easily onto a smaller device, requiring the student to scroll through more than one screen to view the image. At times, navigation is still very difficult. But the information is available and the student can continue his or her research. The

FIGURE 2.2 **Categories of applications used in the past thirty days**

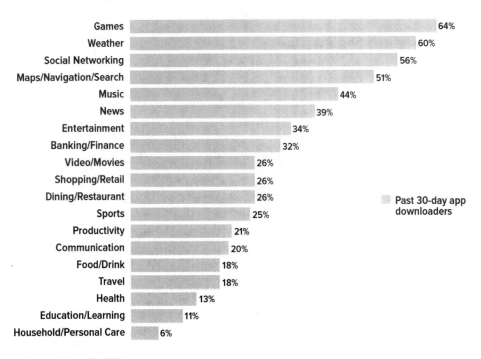

Source: Nielsen (Q2 2011)

major drawback is that looking at information one screen at a time does not give the reader a global view of the topic. Reading a newspaper in print or on a large monitor gives the reader, at a quick glance, an overview of the news for that day. Looking at a smartphone app for the same newspaper generally means choosing a section, whether international, national, local, science, and so forth, and then scrolling through that section, screen after screen, to look at all the articles for that day. Thus a kind of tunnel vision can ensue from using specialized apps on mobile devices, contributing to the Invisible Web. In his article "Using Mobile Devices for Research: Smartphones, Databases, and Libraries," Joe Murphy writes: "There are differences in information-seeking behavior beyond simply reading news on your mobile. What you first use to search often depends upon convenience—and the easiest route is often dictated by your mobile technology habits." He further cautions that "switching gears to professional-grade research as opposed to ready reference or personal trivia questions changes the situation" (Murphy 2010, 14). As the graph in figure 2.2 shows, most research undertaken today is more in the ready reference or trivia category. Students want answers instantaneously, in short bites, and on the go. More in-depth studies are needed to delve further into the information-seeking habits of mobile phone and tablet users.

On the other hand, this new mobile technology will allow students to access library subscription databases from wherever they may be. While this use of the technology is still in its infancy, it will increase as the technology becomes more sophisticated. A huge portion of the Invisible Web is thus opening up to students on new devices, through apps and mobile web browsers. "According to an October 2010 survey conducted by *Library Journal*, 44% of academic libraries and 34% of public libraries offer some type of mobile services" (quoted in De Rosa et al. 2010, 15). Michelle Leigh Jacobs, in her article on libraries and the mobile revolution, writes: "For today's students mobile phones, iPods or MP3 players, are study devices. If we hurry up and get content to them through these mobile devices, we might become just as popular as our computers with internet are" (2009, 288). She calls today's students "the ING (information now generation)" (286). WorldCat offers an iPhone app which provides access to its massive resources and then guides the user to the nearest public library for access to the books ("Mobile Apps for Libraries" 2010). An app from the library vendor Gale, AccessMyLibrary, uses this same GPS capability to access a library within a ten-mile radius of the app user and then allows access to the electronic databases held by Gale at that particular institution ("Mobile" 2010). EBSCOhost, too, has gone mobile by offering access to its databases through a mobile web browser (EBSCOhost 2010, 34–5). Medline is offering a mobile interface to PubMed, although the content is not an exact replica of the online database. In January 2012, Apple introduced new apps and tools to download and use textbooks with the iPad (Chen and Wingfield 2012).

While apps are doing much to expand the visible web, mobile computing can also contribute to the enlargement of the Invisible Web. Aldrich notes that "some search engines such as Google optimize their mobile search engines to provide a limited number of results compared to a full web search" (Aldrich 2010). Joe Murphy cautions that "providing full access without compromising content is an important consideration" (Murphy 2010, 17). In addition, there are new privacy concerns regarding information accessed through mobile phones coupled with location awareness through trackable GPS capabilities. As Timothy Vollmer aptly describes, companies can easily gather "a rich 'digital dossier'" (2010, 4) on what mobile device users access and use. This harks back to the issue of personalization, brought to the forefront by Eli Pariser in his book *The Filter Bubble*. A version of Big Brother looking over the user's shoulder can not only facilitate the customization of information provided by data providers, affecting the objectivity of research, but it can also change the way a wary user searches for that same information. Searching on mobile devices offers the capability to tap Invisible Web content on the go by offering access to an entire smorgasbord of new mobile services. But there is the danger of falling into information silos similar to those described at the beginning of this chapter in the discussion of general-purpose search engines.

New social networking sites and social media are also being used as a marketing tool by librarians to engage with students at their level and to lure them toward resources offered by their institutions. But that does not mean that students utilize these newer forms of communication to engage in academic research. Nonetheless, to keep up with the Google Generation, it behooves library professionals and faculty to follow Joe Murphy's advice: "Think social, real-time, and location-based interaction with content and peers" (Murphy 2010, 18).

The information world has just made a complete circle, from a fully human-centered search process conducted in libraries and focusing on printed books and journals, to an automated function perfected by Google with its PageRank system finding vast amounts of electronic information on the Internet, and now to a social-centered research method where students rely heavily on peers within their social networks and on somewhat narrowly focused mobile apps. Stephen Arnold suggests that "web search may be shifting from brute force spidering and algorithmic text-processing to a more social or human-intermediated service" (Arnold 2010, 21).

What does the picture of information-seeking drawn by the studies reviewed in this chapter portend for today's researchers, particularly student researchers? The studies show that the process is still heavily Googlized, although, as the academic level of students rises, there is greater use of library subscription databases. The introduction of social networking sites such as Facebook has invited friends into the research process. While people have always relied on family and friends for information, the virtual environment changes and expands the pool of people available to be asked.

How will these changes affect the types of resources users find and ultimately use for research? Library offerings—which form the major portion
of the Invisible Web—are not readily part of the equation in the scenario
above. The problem, then, is to introduce the use of the Invisible Web at
an early stage of education. The challenge for educators is to make use of
Invisible Web content second nature at an early age. Can friends help in this
process?

NOTES

1. The twelve studies included in the JISC report are as follows, in chronological order (Connaway and Dickey 2010, 1–2):

   Perceptions of Libraries and Information Resources (OCLC, December
   2005), www.oclc.org/us/en/reports/2005perceptions.htm

   College Students' Perceptions of Libraries and Information Resources
   (OCLC, April 2006), www.oclc.org/us/en/reports/perceptions
   college.htm

   *Sense-Making the Information Confluence: The Whys and Hows of
   College and University User Satisficing of Information Needs* (IMLS/
   Ohio State University/OCLC, July 2006), www.oclc.org/research/
   projects/imls/default.htm

   Researchers and Discovery Services: Behaviour, Perceptions and Needs
   (RIN, November 2006), www.rin.ac.uk/our-work/using-and
   -accessing-information-resources/researchers-and-discovery
   services-behaviour-perc

   Researchers' Use of Academic Libraries and Their Services (RIN/CURL,
   April 2007), www.rin.ac.uk/our-work/using-and-accessing
   -information-resources/researchers-use-academiclibraries-and
   -their-serv

   Information Behaviour of the Researcher of the Future (CIBER/UCL,
   commissioned by BL and JISC, January 2008), www.jisc.ac.uk/
   media/documents/programmemes/reppres/gg_final_keynote
   _11012008.pdf

   *Seeking Synchronicity: Evaluating Virtual Reference Services from User,
   Non-user and Librarian Perspectives* (OCLC/IMLS/Rutgers, June
   2008), www.oclc.org/research/projects/synchronicity/default.htm

   Online Catalogs: What Users and Librarians Want (OCLC, March 2009),
   www.oclc.org/us/en/reports/onlinecatalogs/default.htm 2

E-journals: Their Use, Value and Impact (RIN, April 2009), www.rin.ac
.uk/our-work/communicatingand-disseminating-research/e-journals
-their-use-value-and-impact

*JISC National E-books Observatory Project: Key Findings and Recom-
mendations* (JISC/UCL, November 2009), www.jiscebooksproject
.org

Students' Use of Research Content in Teaching and Learning (JISC,
November 2009), www.jisc.ac.uk/media/documents/aboutus/
workinggroups/studentsuseresearchcontent.pdf

User Behaviour in Resource Discovery (JISC, November 2009),
www.jisc.ac.uk/whatwedo/programmes/inf11/userbehaviour
busandecon.aspx

2. This report was discussed in our previous book, *Going Beyond Google:
The Invisible Web in Teaching and Learning*, published by Neal-Schuman
in 2009.

REFERENCES

Aldrich, Alan W. 2010. "Universities and Libraries Move to the Mobile Web."
EDUCAUSE Quarterly 33, no. 2. www.educause.edu/ero/article/
universities-and-libraries-move-mobile-web.

Arnold, Stephen E. 2010. "Is a Search Revolution Brewing?" *Information Today*
27, no. 6: 20–21. Library, Information Science & Technology Abstracts with
Full Text.

Asher, Andrew, Lynda Duke, and David Green. 2010. "The ERIAL Project: Ethnographic Research in Illinois Academic Libraries." *Academic Commons*, May 17.
http://academiccommons.org/commons/essay/erial-project.

Badke, William. 2009. "The Great Research Disaster." *Online* 33, no. 6: 48–50.
Academic Search Complete.

Chen, Brian X., and Nick Wingfield. 2012. "Apple Introduces Tools to (Someday)
Supplant Print Textbooks." *New York Times*, January 19. http://bits.blogs
.nytimes.com/2012/01/19/apple-unveils-tools-for-digital-textbooks/
?scp=2&sq=apple%20and%20textbooks&st=cse.

Chen, Xiaotian. 2010. "Google Scholar's Dramatic Coverage Improvement Five
Years Later." *Serials Review* 36, no. 4: 221–226. http://dx.doi.org/10.1016/
j.serrev.2010.08.002.

comScore. 2013. "comScore Releases May 2013 U.S. Search Engine Rankings." June 12. www.comscore.com/Insights/Press_Releases/2013/6/comScore_Releases_May_2013_U.S._Search_Engine_Rankings.

Connaway, Lynn Silipigni, and Timothy J. Dickey. 2010. *The Digital Information Seeker: Report of the Findings from Selected OCLC, RIN, and JISC User Behaviour Projects.* London: Higher Education Funding Council for England on behalf of JISC. www.jisc.ac.uk/media/documents/publications/reports/2010/digitalinformationseekerreport.pdf.

Connaway, Lynn Silipigni, Timothy J. Dickey, and Marie L. Radford. 2011. "'If It Is Too Inconvenient I'm Not Going After It': Convenience as a Critical Factor in Information-Seeking Behaviors." *Library & Information Science Research* 33: 179–190. http://dx.doi.org/10.1016/j.lisr.2010.12.002.

De Rosa, Cathy, Joanne Cantrell, Matthew Carlson, Peggy Gallagher, Janet Hawk, and Charlotte Sturtz. 2010. *Perceptions of Libraries, 2010: Context and Community—a Report to the OCLC Membership.* Dublin, OH: OCLC.

Devine, Jane, and Francine Egger-Sider. 2009. *Going Beyond Google: The Invisible Web in Learning and Teaching.* New York: Neal-Schuman.

Du, Jia Tina, and Nina Evans. 2011. "Academic Users' Information Searching on Research Topics: Characteristics of Research Tasks and Search Strategies." *Journal of Academic Librarianship* 37, no. 4: 299–306. http://dx.doi.org/10.1016/j.acalib.2011.04.003.

Dubicki, Eleonora. 2010. "Research Behavior Patterns of Business Students." *Reference Services Review* 38, no. 3: 360–384. http://dx.doi.org/10.1108/00907321011070874.

"EBSCOhost Is Going Mobile." 2010. *Library Times International,* January: 34–35. Library, Information Science & Technology Abstracts with Full Text.

Feuz, Martin, Matthew Fuller, and Felix Stalder. 2011. "Personal Web Searching in the Age of Semantic Capitalism: Diagnosing the Mechanisms of Personalisation." *First Monday* 16, no. 2. http://firstmonday.org/htbin/cgiwrap/bin/ojs/index.php/fm/article/view/3344/2766.

Hampton, Keith N., Lauren Sessions Goulet, Lee Rainie, and Kristen Purcell. 2011. "Social Networking Sites and Our Lives." Pew Internet & American Life Project. http://pewinternet. org/Reports/2011/Technology-and-social-networks.aspx.

Hampton-Reeves, Stuart, Claire Mashiter, Jonathan Westaway, Peter Lumsden, Helen Day, Helen Hewertson, et al. 2009. *Students' Use of Research Content in Teaching and Learning: A Report for the Joint Information Systems Council (JISC)*. Lancashire, UK: Centre for Research-Informed Teaching, University of Central Lancashire. www.jisc.ac.uk/media/documents/aboutus/working groups/studentsuseresearchcontent.pdf.

Hanson, Cody, Heather Hessel, John Barneson, Deborah Boudewyns, Janet Fransen, Lara Friedman-Shedlov, et al. 2009. *Discoverability, Phase 1: Final Report.* Minneapolis, MN: University of Minnesota Libraries. http://conservancy.umn.edu/bitstream/48258/3/DiscoverabilityPhase1Report.pdf.

Hanson, Cody, Heather Hessel, Deborah Boudewyns, Janet Fransen, Lara Friedman-Shedlov, Stephen Hearn, et al. 2010. *Discoverability, Phase 2: Final Report.* Minneapolis, MN: University of Minnesota Libraries. http://conservancy.umn.edu/bitstream/99734/3/DiscoverabilityPhase2ReportFull.pdf.

Hargittai, Eszter, Lindsay Fullerton, Ericka Menchen-Trevino, and Kristin Yates Thomas. 2010. "Trust Online: Young Adults' Evaluation of Web Content." *International Journal of Communication* 4: 468–494. http://ijoc.org/ojs/index.php/ijoc/article/view/636.

Harris, Robert. 2010. "Evaluating Internet Research Sources." *VirtualSalt.* www.virtualsalt.com/evalu8it.htm.

Head, Alison J., and Michael B. Eisenberg. 2009. *Lessons Learned: How College Students Seek Information in the Digital Age.* Seattle, WA: Project Information Literacy, December 1. http://projectinfolit.org/pdfs/PIL_Fall2009_Year1 Report_12_2009.pdf.

———. 2010a. *Truth Be Told: How College Students Evaluate and Use Information in the Digital Age.* Seattle, WA: Project Information Literacy, November 1. http://projectinfolit.org/pdfs/PIL_Fall2010_Survey_FullReport1.pdf.

———. 2010b. "How Today's College Students Use *Wikipedia* for Course-Related Research." *First Monday* 15, no. 3. www.firstmonday.org/htbin/cgiwrap/bin/ojs/index.php/fm/article/view/2830/2476.

———. 2011. "How College Students Use the Web to Conduct Everyday Life Research. *First Monday* 16, no. 4. http://firstmonday.org/htbin/cgiwrap/bin/ojs/index.php/fm/article/view/3484/2857.

Horling, Bryan, and Matthew Kulick. 2009. "Personalized Search for Everyone." *The Official Google Blog,* December 4. http://googleblog.blogspot.com/2009/12/personalized-search-for-everyone.html.

Jacobs, Michelle Leigh. 2009. "Libraries and the Mobile Revolution: Remediation=Relevance." *Reference Services Review* 37, no. 3: 286–290. http://dx.doi.org/10.1108/00907320910982776.

Jacobsen, Wade C., and Renata Forste. 2011. "The Wired Generation: Academic and Social Outcomes of Electronic Media Use among University Students." *Cyberpsychology, Behavior, and Social Networking* 14, no. 5: 275–280. http://dx.doi.org/10.1089/cyber.2010.0135.

Jacsó, Péter. 2011. "Google Scholar Duped and Deduped: The Aura of 'Robometrics.'" *Online Information Review* 35, no. 1: 154–160. http://dx.doi.org/10.1108/14684521111113632.

Jones, Edgar. 2010. "Google Books as a General Research Collection." *Library Resources & Technical Services* 54, no. 2: 77–89. Library, Information Science & Technology Abstracts with Full Text.

Judd, Terry, and Gregor Kennedy. 2011. "Expediency-Based Practice? Medical Students' Reliance on Google and Wikipedia for Biomedical Inquiries." *British Journal of Educational Technology* 42, no. 2: 351–360. http://dx.doi.org/10.1111/j.1467-8535.2009.01019.x.

Kim, Kyung-Sun, EunYoung Yoo-Lee, and Sei-Ching Joanna Sin. 2011. "Social Media as Information Source: Undergraduates' Use and Evaluation Behavior." Poster presented at the ASIS&T annual conference in New Orleans, October 9–12. www.asis.org/asist2011/posters/283_FINAL_SUBMISSION.pdf.

Kingsley, Karl, Gillian M. Galbraith, Matthew Herring, Eva Stowers, Tanis Stewart, and Karla V. Kingsley. 2011. "Why Not Just Google It? An Assessment of Information Literacy Skills in a Biomedical Science Curriculum." *BMC Medical Education* 11, no. 17: 1–8. http://dx.doi.org/10.1186/1472-6920-11-17.

Lewandowski, Dirk. 2010. "Google Scholar as a Tool for Discovering Journal Articles in Library and Information Science." *Online Information Review* 34, no. 2: 250–262. http://dx.doi.org/10.1108/14684521011036972.

McCracken, Harry. 2013. "Who's Winning, iOS or Android? All the Numbers, All in One Place." *Time Tech*, April 16. http://techland.time.com/2013/04/16/ios-vs-android.

McDonnell, Michael, and Ali Shiri. 2011. "Social Search: A Taxonomy of, and a User-Centred Approach to, Social Web Search." *Program: Electronic Library and Information Systems* 45, no. 1: 6–28. http://dx.doi.org/10.1108/00330331111107376.

Mellow, John P., Jr. 2011. "Total Apps Available for Android and iPhone May Have Reached One Million." *Macworld* (blog), September 19. www.macworld.co.uk/mac-creative/news/index.cfm?newsid=3304234.

Merriam-Webster Online. 2011. S.v. "google." Accessed October 6. www.merriam-webster.com/dictionary/google.

"Mobile Apps for Libraries." 2010. *Libraryland Roundup* (blog), Friday, April 9. http://librarylandroundup.blogspot.com/2010/04/mobile-apps-for-libraries .html.

Murphy, Joe. 2010. "Using Mobile Devices for Research: Smartphones, Databases, and Libraries." *Online* 34, no. 3: 14–18. Academic Search Complete.

Nicholas, David, and Ian Rowlands. 2011. "Social Media Use in the Research Work-flow." *Information Services & Use* 31, no. 1–2: 61–83. http://dx.doi.org/10.3233/ ISU-2011-0623.

Nicholas, David, Ian Rowlands, David Clark, Thomas Nicholas, and Hamid R. Jamali. 2010. *Scholarly Digital Use and Information-Seeking Behaviour in Business and Economics: An Evidence-Based Study.* JISC User Behaviour Observational Study, June 30. London: Higher Education Funding Council for England on behalf of JISC. www.jisc.ac.uk/media/documents/publications/ programme/2010/ubirdciber2010.pdf.

Nicholas, David, Ian Rowlands, David Clark, and Peter Williams. 2011. "Google Generation II: Web Behaviour Experiments with the BBC." *Aslib Proceedings: New Information Perspectives* 63, no. 1: 28–45. http://dx.doi.org/10.1108/ 00012531111103768.

Nielsen. 2010. "The State of Mobile Apps." *NielsenWire* (blog), June 1. http://blog.nielsen.com/nielsenwire/online_mobile/the-state-of-mobile-apps.

———. 2011. "Mobile Apps Beat the Mobile Web Among US Android Smartphone Users." *NielsenWire*, August 18. www.nielsen.com/us/en/newswire/2011/ mobile-apps-beat-the-mobile-web-among-us-android-smartphone-users.html.

———. 2012. *State of the Media: The Social Media Report.* Nielsen. www.nielsen .com/content/dam/corporate/us/en/reports-downloads/2012-Reports/ The-Social-Media-Report-2012.pdf.

Niu, Xi, Bradley M. Hemminger, Cory Lown, Stephanie Adams, Cecelia Brown, Allison Level, et al. 2010. "National Study of Information Seeking Behavior of Academic Researchers in the United States." *Journal of the American Society for Information Science and Technology* 61, no. 5: 869–890. http:// dx.doi.org/10.1002/asi.21307.

Pariser, Eli. 2011. *The Filter Bubble: What the Internet Is Hiding from You.* New York: Penguin.

Prensky, Marc. H. 2001. "Digital Natives, Digital Immigrants." *On the Hori-zon* 9, no. 5. www.marcprensky.com/writing/Prensky%20-%20Digital%20 Natives,%20Digital%20Immigrants%20-%20Part1.pdf.

Purcell, Kristen. 2011. "Search and Email Still Top the List of Most Popular Online Activities." Pew Internet & Life American Project, August 9. http://pewinternet .org/~/media/Files/Reports/2011/PIP_Search-and-Email.pdf.

Rowlands, Ian, David Nicholas, Bill Russell, Nicholas Canty, and Anthony Watkinson. 2011. "Social Media Use in the Research Workflow." *Learned Publishing* 24, no. 3: 183–195. http://dx.doi.org/10.1087/20110306.

Silver, David. 2011. "Twitter Meets the Breakfast Club." *Chronicle of Higher Education*, May 13: B33–B34. LexisNexis Academic.

Smith, Aaron. 2011. "13% of Online Adults Use Twitter." Pew Internet & American Life Project., June 1. http://pewinternet.org/~/media/Files/Reports/2011/Twitter%20Update%202011.pdf.

Smith, Shannon D., and Judith Borreson Caruso. 2010. *The ECAR Study of Undergraduate Students and Information Technology, 2010*. Boulder, CO: EDUCAUSE. http://net.educause.edu/ir/library/pdf/ERS1006/RS/ERS1006W.pdf.

Stalder, Felix, and Christine Mayer. 2009. "The Second Index: Search Engines, Personalization and Surveillance." In *Deep Search: The Politics of Search Beyond Google*, edited by Konrad Becker and Felix Stalder, 98–105. Innsbruck: Studien Verlag.

Tapscott, Don. 2008. *Grown Up Digital: How the Net Generation Is Changing Your World*. New York: McGraw-Hill.

Taylor, Paul, and Scott Keeter, eds. 2010. *Millennials: A Portrait of Generation Next, Confident, Connected, Open to Change*. Pew Research Center. http://pewsocial trends.org/files/2010/10/millennials-confident-connected-open-to-change.pdf.

UCL (University College London). 2008. *Information Behaviour of the Researcher of the Future: A CIBER Briefing Paper*. [Executive summary.] University College London/Centre for Information Behaviour and the Evaluation of Research [CIBER], January 11. www.ucl.ac.uk/infostudies/research/ciber/downloads/ggexecutive.pdf.

———. [2011]. *Google Generation Research at University College London*. www.ucl .ac.uk/infostudies/research/ciber/GG2.pdf.

Vaidhyanathan, Siva. 2011. *The Googlization of Everything (and Why We Should Worry)*. Berkeley: University of California Press.

Vollmer, Timothy. 2010. *There's an App for That! Libraries and Mobile Technology: An Introduction to Public Policy Considerations*. Washington, DC: American Library Association Office for Information Technology Policy. www.ala.org/ala/aboutala/offices/oitp/publications/policybriefs/mobiledevices.pdf.

Walters, William H. 2009. "Google Scholar Search Performance: Comparative Recall and Precision." *portal: Libraries and the Academy* 9, no. 1: 5–24. http://dx.doi.org/10.1353/pla.0.0034.

Wong, William, Hanna Stelmaszewska, Nazlin Bhimani, Sukhbinder Barn, and Balbir Barn. 2009. *User Behaviour in Resource Discovery: Final Report.* JISC User Behaviour Observational Study, November. London: Higher Education Funding Council for England on behalf of JISC. www.ubird.mdx.ac.uk/wp-content/uploads/2009/11/ubird-report-final.pdf.

Young, Jeffrey R. 2009. "Teaching with Twitter: Not for the Faint of Heart." *Chronicle of Higher Education*, November 22. LexisNexis Academic.

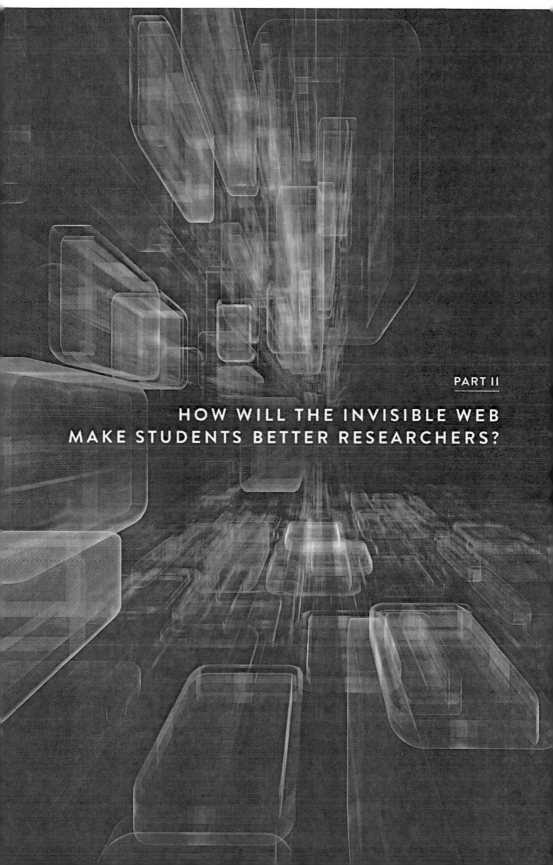

PART II

HOW WILL THE INVISIBLE WEB
MAKE STUDENTS BETTER RESEARCHERS?

TEACHING THE INVISIBLE WEB: A SURVEY OF THEORY AND PRACTICE

Johnny, this is the Invisible Web, Invisible Web, this is Johnny.
Survey response to "How do you introduce the Invisible Web when teaching?"

NIMATED BY THE CONVICTION THAT THE Invisible Web should be taught to all students because it would make them better researchers, we took two steps to find out the actual state of Invisible Web teaching today. The first step was to contact experts who have written about the Invisible Web and ask them to comment on the need to teach it. The second step was to conduct an anonymous online survey, directed at professional librarians and educators around the world. The results of these activities are discussed in this chapter; the implications of the survey results for teaching will be covered in chapter 4.

SHOULD THE INVISIBLE WEB BE TAUGHT?

Some might argue that the Invisible Web need not be taught because search engines provide enough information already. Or they might say that the Invisible Web is difficult to teach, that there is barely enough time to teach the other important aspects of research, and that everyone has been getting along well enough without it. Some of these same people believe that the search engine industry will eventually make all information, including Invisible Web resources, accessible and that, therefore, instruction about the Invisible Web is probably a waste of time or, at best, an interim measure. It is not clear, however, that the search engine companies have sufficient incentive to resolve all Invisible Web issues, since these companies currently make their revenue from advertising, not from search. On the other hand, some individuals may rise to the challenge and become research specialists. Companies and others in need of information could simply leave in-depth research to these specialists and, when pressed, concede that help is available—at a price—if and when needed.

But can it really be that difficult to teach about research and the Invisible Web? And is it worth the risk of creating a digital divide between those who learn about how to mine the Invisible Web and those who do not? We have always felt that everyone would benefit from learning about the Invisible Web, and we have found that many other people agree. We believe the Invisible Web can easily be taught as part of any research or information literacy program in schools at every level. Teaching about the Invisible Web is really only about giving a more complete picture of the information world. In support of our cause, we asked colleagues who have studied and written about the Invisible Web to comment on whether there is a need to teach it to students. Here are some of their responses.

Yazdan Mansourian, quoted in chapter 1 about the cognitive definition of the Invisible Web, had this to say about teaching the Invisible Web (e-mail, July 9, 2011):

> Yes, I think we should teach our students about the Invisible Web and about all the causal reasons of information invisibility. Because, most of them are not very familiar with the process of information storage and retrieval on the Web, and they sometimes overestimate the effectiveness of general purpose search engines. My teaching experiences, as a university lecturer, show they basically trust Google and the other popular search engines and believe whatever these tools offer them in their result list is the only answer to their questions. They also mainly believe if something exists on the Web there is no reason that Google cannot find it! Therefore if they do not find what they are looking for, then it probably does not exist. Furthermore, they have a sort of

simplistic view about the relevance ranking in these tools. As a result, they mostly suppose the first page of the search result should inevitably have the most relevant documents that they need. Nevertheless, as you know, the notion of "relevance" is very contextual and conceptual and search tools are not necessarily as successful as we wish in ranking the relevant results.

In summary, I think our students should learn that as a result of the enormity and diversity of information resources on the Web, looking for the best answer to their questions on this ever-increasing ocean is not a very simple and straightforward procedure. Therefore, they firstly need to enhance their information literacy skills and secondly learn about the basic mechanism of information storage and retrieval on the Web. They should be aware of the major strengths and weaknesses of Web-based search tools. Therefore, we hopefully will be able to provide them with a more holistic and realistic picture of the information retrieval process on the Web.

Wendy Boswell, author of *The About.com Guide to Online Research*, expressed a similar view (e-mail, July 27, 2011):

In my experience, as I've watched search engines and searchers for the last ten years, search skills have actually regressed. It's true—after all, why do Web searchers need to know how to do a simple Boolean search or even put their searches in quotation marks when search engines intuitively know what they're looking for even before they've finished typing it?

However, this doesn't eliminate the need for a basic Web search skill set, and it certainly does not erase the fact that there is still a vastly underused Web of knowledge out there that 99% of Web searchers don't even know exists. In addition, it also doesn't mean that search results are going to be anything close to relevant. Algorithms will never substitute for human intelligence and intuition.

. . . I think the Invisible Web and learning about it, as well as advanced search techniques, are so important. A cursory search engine query is about as deep as many Web users are ever going to get, but if they could actually visualize the vast resources that are available to them, I think it would be a very attractive prospect.

Maureen Henninger, author of *The Hidden Web*, wrote about the Invisible Web's importance for knowledge workers especially (e-mail, July 27, 2011):

> Search engine technologies and partnerships are bringing more of the invisible web to the surface and for the average information-seeker the fact that there is an invisible web is possibly not important. However, I still believe that all students need to be information-literate and should be made aware of the vast amount of resources available on the Internet. However for students who are moving into information-intensive professions, e.g. researchers, investigative journalists, information managers, etc. formal teaching about the invisible web is essential.

Karen R. Diaz, author of the article "The Invisible Web: Navigating the Web outside Traditional Search Engines," emphasized the shifting nature of the Invisible Web (e-mail, August 1, 2011):

> Part of the "problem" is economic, political, and legal so technology can't solve all the problems. Technology advances have changed the problem. In some respects they have alleviated the issue, and, as indicated in the personalization issue above, some advances in the technology have brought about new problems in regards to discovery. . . .
>
> I think that education about the invisible web needs to emphasize that this is an evolving issue, that it's not easy to clearly define what's invisible and what's not, and that something that is visible today might be invisible tomorrow.

Laura Cohen, author of the web guide *Internet Tutorials* (www.web .archive.org/web/20130062015752/http://internettutorials.net/deepweb .asp, placed an emphasis on databases in her response (e-mail, July 8, 2011):

> I do share the concern that people don't know about the Invisible Web. Because general search engines have integrated a growing amount of Invisible Web content into their results, it is easy to believe that "everything" is available through these tools. But this is far from the case.
>
> Yes! Students are a prime population for learning about the Invisible Web. To achieve academic success, students need to learn how to

do in-depth, scholarly research using a variety of high quality sources. Some material is available on the free Web, but there is much more of value that students need to be familiar with and to use. This is where academic libraries come into play. Academic libraries are purveyors of an enormous amount of material on the Invisible Web in the form of the many databases and e-journals they have purchased for scholarly use.

The experts that we consulted were, with one exception, supportive of teaching the Invisible Web. True, they were all approached because of their publications on the subject, which already attested to their interest in and support of the topic. The lone dissenter, Ellis Horowitz, coauthor of the article "Indexing the Invisible Web: A Survey" (Ru and Horowitz 2005), was optimistic about the progress being made by search engines (e-mail, August 8, 2011):

> Google (and other search engines) appear to me to be doing an adequate job identifying online databases that may contain relevant information in response to some query. And some online database sites do make special efforts to get their dynamic pages indexed.
>
> In the future I believe that search engines will try (and be able) to answer far more sophisticated questions than what can be expressed in two or three words. This will necessitate a deeper understanding of the relationships among data residing at different websites, including deep websites. The next few years should see major improvements in search engines.

Horowitz's optimism will undoubtedly be warranted someday, but can we afford to leave students in the dark until then?

INVISIBLE WEB SURVEY

To begin the exploration of how to teach the Invisible Web, we drafted a survey to gain some insights into what educators and librarians know about the Invisible Web and how they use it. During the summer of 2011, we administered the survey to check the pulse, if any, of that concept. We wanted to learn if teachers, academics, and librarians in school, academic, and public libraries talked about the Invisible Web. Was the Invisible Web being taught and, if yes, under what circumstances? The survey was intended not only to produce data but also to create an opportunity for dialogue with colleagues all over the world in the education and library professions. The survey consisted of twelve questions (see appendix) and was administered anonymously via SurveyMonkey. It was posted to electronic discussion lists for librarians and educators and reached people in North America, Europe, Australia, New Zealand, South Africa, and Hong Kong. Over 1,000 responses were received.

The survey consisted of two parts. The first five questions were intended to gather information about familiarity with the Invisible Web. In the second part, questions 6 to 11 targeted issues about teaching the Invisible Web. The final question thanked the participants and solicited additional comments.

PART ONE:
WHAT DO EDUCATORS AND LIBRARIANS KNOW ABOUT THE INVISIBLE WEB?

Questions 1 and 2: Do you know about the Invisible Web? If not, do you want to know more?

Of the 1,019 who responded to this question, 64% (652) answered that they knew about the Invisible Web and the rest, 36% (367), answered that they did not (fig. 3.1). Were they interested in knowing more about the Invisible Web? Of the 584 people who answered this question, 91% (531) said that they would like to know more, and 9% (53) said they would not. Those answering no were thanked for their participation and taken to the end of the survey.

FIGURE 3.1 **Do you know about the Invisible Web? (*n* = 1,019)**

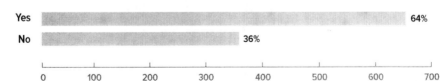

Source: Invisible Web/Deep Web/Hidden Web survey, question 1 (see appendix).

Question 3: How would you define the Invisible Web?

With question 3, we wanted to learn what people generally understood the Invisible Web to be. Most of the 568 respondents to this question offered the essential elements of the definition as shown in figure 3.2. As respondents could include multiple concepts in their definitions, the percentages listed in figure 3.2 will add up to more than 100%.

FIGURE 3.2 **How would you define the Invisible Web? (*n* = 568)**

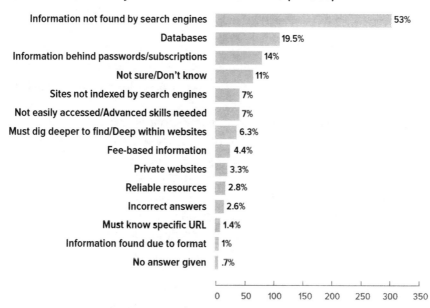

Information not found by search engines	53%
Databases	19.5%
Information behind passwords/subscriptions	14%
Not sure/Don't know	11%
Sites not indexed by search engines	7%
Not easily accessed/Advanced skills needed	7%
Must dig deeper to find/Deep within websites	6.3%
Fee-based information	4.4%
Private websites	3.3%
Reliable resources	2.8%
Incorrect answers	2.6%
Must know specific URL	1.4%
Information found due to format	1%
No answer given	.7%

Source: Invisible Web/Deep Web/Hidden Web survey, question 3 (see appendix).

Here is a summary of the responses to question 3:

- The majority of people defined the Invisible Web as material not found by using search engines. Google provided the standard for search engines, as it was listed more times than any other when a specific tool was mentioned at all.
- The next most common response was that the Invisible Web represented database content (19.5%).
- A small percentage of responses, 7% (39), emphasized that Invisible Web materials are not easily found and require advanced search skills. Such a response implies that more teaching about the Invisible Web is needed.
- The responses show a distinction between those who said that Invisible Web materials are not found by search engines and those

who wrote that the materials are not *indexed* by search engines. We interpreted indexing to refer to the way that a search engine identifies sites and is constructed. Indexing was mentioned in more technical answers and grouped with linking issues (search engine spiders follow links from one site to another) as well as no-indexing protocols, which prevent search engines from indexing a site and making it available as part of search results.

- Other factors that contribute to the Invisible Web and that were mentioned to a lesser degree, such as fees and passwords, are all relevant to the definition but fail to represent a complete picture of the Invisible Web.
- Only sixteen responses specifically defined Invisible Web resources with a value statement. Across these answers were references to reliability, accuracy, "gems of information," and "good stuff." There were no negative statements.
- Of all the 502 people who offered correct definitions of the Invisible Web, 304 (60%) offered only one concept in their definition. The other 198 (40%) gave more complex definitions with multiple concepts. Survey forms almost always seem to encourage brevity, and that may explain some of the single-concept answers. However, it may also point to a real need for teaching the complex reasons for material falling into the Invisible Web.

Question 4: Have you used it in your own research?

Over half of the 682 people responding to question 4, or 383 (56%), reported using the Invisible Web in their own research (fig. 3.3). This figure is a smaller percentage than the 64% who had stated that they knew about the Invisible Web. This difference may be due to the fact that relatively few people (19.5%) equated the Invisible Web with databases (question 3, figure 3.2). Anyone

FIGURE 3.3 Have you used the Invisible Web in your own research? (*n* = 682)

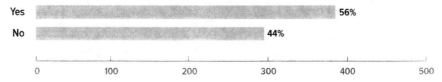

Source: Data from Invisible Web/Deep Web/Hidden Web survey, question 4 (see appendix).

doing research usually has to make use of subscription databases offered through a public or academic institution, if for nothing else than a literature review. Nonetheless, of those people who know about the Invisible Web, almost all have used it in their own research—a strong endorsement for teaching about the Invisible Web to anyone who has to conduct research.

Question 5: How did you learn about the Invisible Web?

Question 5 included six possible answers: journal articles, books, presentations/workshops, course work, colleagues, and other. Each of the 496 respondents could choose more than one category, so the percentages listed will equal more than 100%. Their answers are charted in figure 3.4.

FIGURE 3.4 **How did you learn about the Invisible Web? (***n* = 496)

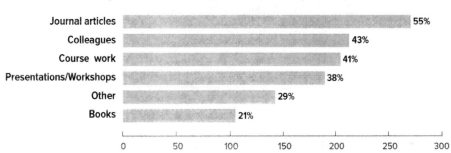

Source: Invisible Web/Deep Web/Hidden Web survey, question 5 (see appendix).

It is interesting to note that only 41% of respondents to question 5 mentioned learning about the Invisible Web in course work. These respondents may represent more recent graduates. Many of the participants, of course, may have gone through their course work before the potential of the web as a research tool was developed or realized. With the systematic introduction of the Invisible Web in schools, this number would naturally increase.

Many respondents (169) included "other" in their answers and wrote additional comments which indicated that they had learned about the Invisible Web through various professional development activities such as blogs, on the job, or from their own research experiences. Thirty-two of these responses simply listed the first five categories in question 5 and were thus added to the percentages for those categories. This left 137 responses (29%) in the category "other." These 137 responses are enumerated in table 3.1.

TABLE 3.1

Additional comments to question 5
(How did you learn about the Invisible Web?)

Response	Number (*n* = 137)	%
From the survey	34	25%
From professional blogs, LISTSERVs, etc.	23	17%
Don't know what the Invisible Web is	22	16%
As part of work	16	11.6%
From my own research experience	15	11%
As part of formal education	8	6%
"I googled it"	7	5%
Other	5	3.6%
By accident	3	2.2%
From databases	3	2.2%
From a librarian	1	0.7%

Source: Invisible Web/Deep Web/Hidden Web survey, question 5 (see appendix).

Analysis of Part One of the Survey

There are a number of conclusions that we can draw from the results of the answers to the first five questions of the survey.

- Overall, in the first part of the survey, the biggest surprise was that only 19.5% of the respondents to question 3 equated the Invisible Web with databases, whereas 64% of respondents to question 1 indicated that they knew about the Invisible Web. We were surprised that more educators and librarians did not make this correlation between databases and the Invisible Web, especially when it should form a natural part of the process of introducing students to subscription databases.

- On the other hand, the majority of respondents did indicate in their definition of the Invisible Web that it consists of information not found by Google and other search engines. Many, however, did not elaborate or give any additional information on what it is that the search engines cannot find. What emerges from this analysis is that the core of every lesson about the Invisible Web has to focus on what it is that is invisible.

- We acknowledge that some self-selection took place at the time of filling out the survey. Even if they had never before encountered the concept of the Invisible Web, respondents felt curious enough to continue with the survey. Indeed, in question 5, thirty-four people acknowledged that they had actually learned about the Invisible Web through the survey itself! Although that was never our intent, it can be considered a good side-effect, definitely contributing to the dialogue in a way that we had not anticipated.

- Finally, only sixteen people expressed anything in their definitions for question 3 about the value of the information or of the websites that constitute the Invisible Web. A better job needs to be done to explain the Invisible Web in terms of the value of its content and what it has to offer to researchers. As searching the Invisible Web does require more effort than a simple Google search, the argument needs to be made that the results are well worth that effort.

PART TWO: HOW ARE LIBRARIANS AND EDUCATORS TEACHING ABOUT THE INVISIBLE WEB?

Question 6: Do you teach about the Invisible Web?

With the crucial issue of whether the Invisible Web is taught, the balance tipped toward the negative, with 363 respondents (56.6%) saying that they did not teach about the Invisible Web (fig. 3.5). It is possible that educators present today's information world as consisting of the web, search engines, and library subscription databases without ever naming the Invisible Web or mentioning other resources not found by search engines. However, it is just as likely that even a simple enumeration of such resources is never brought up. It is interesting to note that the ratio of people who answered this ques-

FIGURE 3.5 Do you teach about the Invisible Web? (n = 642)

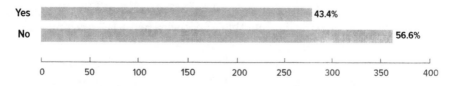

Source: Invisible Web/Deep Web/Hidden Web survey, question 6 (see appendix).

tion to those who did not is nearly two to one (642 to 381); that is, more than a third of respondents avoided answering the question—surely not those who do teach the Invisible Web in their classes. Some librarians and faculty who have never taught a class or a course about the Invisible Web, or have not integrated the concept into a lecture on research, may have felt more comfortable skipping the question altogether rather than having to admit, even to themselves, that they are not dealing with this crucial segment of research.

Question 4 (Have you used the Invisible Web in your own research?) and question 6 (Do you teach about the Invisible Web?) can easily be cross-tabulated. The results are as follows: Of those who have used the Invisible Web in their own research (383), slightly over 90% teach it. Of those who have taught the Invisible Web (279), close to 67% use it in their own research. The correlation between knowing about the Invisible Web (question 1) and teaching about it (question 6) is the strongest. Of the people who answered yes to the question of whether they know about the Invisible Web (652), over 97% also answered yes to question 6: thus 97% teach it in some fashion. This is a strong endorsement of the value of teaching about the Invisible Web: those who know about the Invisible Web consider it worth teaching, or vice-versa: they know about the Invisible Web because they teach it. Their teaching, in turn, brings important awareness to students conducting research.

Question 7: Do you think that students should be taught about the Invisible Web?

Out of 521 respondents, 78% agreed with the statement that the Invisible Web should be taught. Only 15 people (2.8%) answered in the negative. More, 41 (8%), expressed doubt, either because they simply did not know what the Invisible Web represents or they were not sure whether it should be taught. A few, 26 (5%), answered "probably." The breakdown can be seen in figure 3.6.

As part of question 7, we also asked respondents to explain why (or why not). The most prevalent reason offered for teaching about the Invisible Web was to combat students' assumption that they can find everything using Google. As it is in so many other contexts, Google was simply named, almost as a generic term; there seems to be little effort anymore to use the truly generic term *search engine*. This finding mirrors what Scott Cleland said recently: "For a growing percentage of users, Google is the Internet" (quoted in Hatch 2011, 958). Teachers and librarians are well aware of students' inclination to start and end their research with Google

FIGURE 3.6 Should students be taught about the Invisible Web? (*n* = 521)

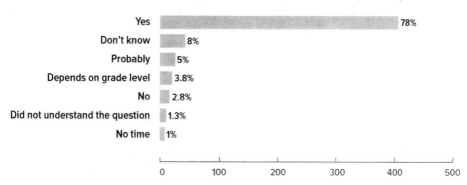

Source: Invisible Web/Deep Web/Hidden Web survey, question 7 (see appendix).

regardless of the array of subscription databases offered by their educational institutions.

An interesting point that emerged from survey question 7 is that 2% of respondents who answered yes, that students should be taught about the Invisible Web, wrote that, while they do cover the concept of the Invisible Web in their teaching, they do not actually use the term. The following comments are illustrative of this:

- "I don't really call it the Invisible Web, but rather library databases or subscription databases paid for via tuition (that gets a lot of response)."
- "I don't say 'Invisible Web.' I show them databases."
- "I don't call it the Invisible Web. I start by asking students whether they think they will want to go on to further education after school. The majority do and so I tell them that Google won't be enough to get a pass."
- "I don't talk about it as 'the invisible web.' I talk a lot about scholarly information and where you will find it and why."
- "I know some people worry that we confuse students by discussing the invisible web."

One person felt that the duality to be emphasized should be between paid and free resources rather than visible or invisible and that the term "Invisible Web" was intimidating. Someone else called it passé.

One person thought that awareness was enough.

A few people (1%) answered yes, they would like to introduce the concept of the Invisible Web to their students but have no time to do so. Others (3.8%) felt that when to introduce it would depend on grade levels.

It is interesting to highlight a few sample responses to the question whether the Invisible Web should be taught.

- "I think high school students should know that it exists and have some easy practice searching something like ejournals or conference proceedings. College students should have more practice and understand that general search engines are not searching the entire content of the World Wide Web. Graduate students should become much more familiar with it and assignments should include lists of relevant search engines and types of resources available in their area of study. This knowledge would better prepare them for professional life outside of school."
- "Yes, my philosophy is that everyone is a life-long learner and everyone should know about as many resources as possible. As soon as students are taught to use the internet, they should be taught about what's not indexed by search engines."
- "It is all too easy to equate 'Google' with the entire universe of online information, especially (I suspect) for the 'digital natives' though in fact even for information professionals."
- "I teach about the invisible web to help break students out of the google-only search mentality. I specifically discuss the layers of the internet to show them the true vastness of the online information world."

Question 8: In what circumstances do you teach about the Invisible Web or would you teach about it if given the opportunity?

Respondents were encouraged to give as many answers as applied to this question, so the number of answers was high (1,275) in proportion to the number of people who participated (478). The percentages given in figure 3.7 represent the proportion in relationship to the number of answers.

The most prevalent scenario in which educators teach about the Invisible Web is the one-shot class presentation, also known as "bibliographic instruction" (n = 332, 26%), followed closely by the reference desk, where instruction is given on a one-to-one basis (*n* = 291, 23%). These were followed by workshops, tutorials, courses taught for credit, and other. Answers given under other are shown in table 3.2, where percentages represent the proportion of the 55 total responses.

FIGURE 3.7 In what circumstances do you teach about the Invisible Web? (*n* = 1,275 total responses)

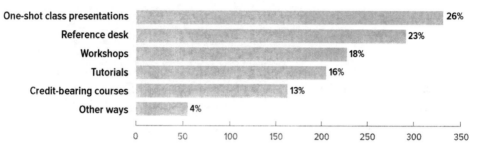

Source: Invisible Web/Deep Web/Hidden Web survey, question 8 (see appendix).

TABLE 3.2

Additional comments to question 8
(In what circumstances do you teach about the Invisible Web?)

Response	Number (*n* = 55)	%
Staff orientation/workshops/training/ professional development	8	15%
Online guides/LibGuides	5	9%
Links	4	7%
Share with others	4	7%
Handouts	1	1.8%
Library book	1	1.8%
Social networking site	1	1.8%
Library website	1	1.8%
Depends on circumstances	2	3.6%
As part of assessment	1	1.8%
All of the above	1	1.8%
Not sure/Don't know	5	9%
Don't teach	9	16%
N/A	12	22%

Source: Invisible Web/Deep Web/Hidden Web survey, question 8 (see appendix).

Some comments offered for question 8 are informative. The comments that repeated the categories from figure 3.7 were pulled out of table 3.2 and incorporated into figure 3.7. What is left are answers that did not fit into any of the given five choices. Eight respondents noted that they give or would like to give training, workshops, or orientations to faculty on this topic. This is crucial, as librarians and a select few faculty cannot hope to fully impart this idea of the Invisible Web in one-shot instruction classes or one-to-one at the reference desk alone. The Invisible Web is a concept that has to be reinforced with every research paper assigned in every class.

Others (n = 5) mentioned an online component of teaching about the Invisible Web, with the greater use of online guides and tutorials such as LibGuides. A quick search of the LibGuides Community site (www .libguides.com) on July 12, 2013, listed 88 guides under "Invisible Web," another 68 under "Deep Web," and 89 under "Hidden Web." The guides represented both subject courses and library websites at many grade levels. This proliferation of materials speaks to the existence of a community of educators who are introducing the Invisible Web to their students.

Nine respondents to question 8 said that they don't teach the Invisible Web, another five responded that they were not sure or did not know how to answer this question, and twelve said that the question did not apply to their situations.

Question 9: How do you introduce the Invisible Web when teaching?

In answer to question 9, one respondent wrote, "Johnny, this is the Invisible Web, Invisible Web, this is Johnny." We really appreciated the intended humor and wish it were that easy.

When it is taught, the Invisible Web most often forms part of an introduction to search engines (mentioned by 12% of respondents) or to databases (11%). See figure 3.8. Both are logical opportunities for discussing available sources, whether they come from the surface web or the Invisible Web, and the limits of search engines.

A selection of answers to question 9 provides a variety of teaching ideas. Some respondents (n = 12, 3.3%) show examples of Invisible Web sources; others seize opportunities provided by specific assignments (n = 8, 2.2%); a few (n = 11, 3.1%) formulate questions designed to ensure that students use Invisible Web resources. Other approaches are more passive (e.g., some simply provide links to Invisible Web guides; n = 6, 1.6%), or limited (e.g.,

FIGURE 3.8 **How do you introduce the Invisible Web when teaching?** (*n* = 353)

Category	Percentage
Do not teach it	26.3%
In discussion of search engines	12%
When introducing databases	11%
Explain it	6.7%
As part of Internet searching	6.5%
In a class on research	6.2%
With a graphic	4.2%
On an individual basis	4%
When comparing Google with databases	4%
Show examples of it	3.3%
Use questions to force use	3.1%
In discussion of evaluation	2.5%
In conjunction with an assignment	2.2%
As advanced searching	2%
Provide links to information	1.6%
Other answers	3.4%

Source: Invisible Web/Deep Web/Hidden Web survey, question 9 (see appendix).

two respondents who answered "other" only discuss the Invisible Web when teaching about primary source materials).

One respondent described a public library course on the "Deep Web" for adults. Several people thought the Invisible Web could be taught as a class within a course. Two respondents felt the Invisible Web should not be taught at the community college level.

One rather lukewarm answer was that "awareness should be enough"; there is no need to teach it: suffice it to mention the Invisible Web within the context of information. Several answers alluded to the concept of information literacy and how the Invisible Web can be brought into that conversation. But the consensus seemed to be that it was more important to focus on the evaluation of information in general, rather than categorize web resources as visible or invisible.

Considering how question 9 is worded, it is surprising how many respondents said that they do not teach the Invisible Web at all (*n* = 93, 26.3%; cf. fig. 3.5). It is unclear why they answered this question in the first place.

The next two chapters will address ways to introduce the Invisible Web in teaching.

Question 10: Do you think that learning about the Invisible Web helps students with their research?

An underlying theme of this book is how to make students better researchers, so question 10 is of paramount importance. Figure 3.9 represents the analysis of the open-ended responses to question 10. Overwhelmingly, the respondents (70% of them) consider that knowing about the Invisible Web helps students with their research. One answer captures the essence of most yes responses: "Yes, in that it helps them understand information, its organization and the importance of evaluating [it]." One respondent went so far as to describe learning about the Invisible Web as the basis for information literacy in general: "Introducing the invisible web prior to a research project allows students to compare search results using search engines, subject directories and databases. Through this process, students learn naturally how to evaluate a source to determine its credibility." Another person responded that "finding valuable reliable information is the key to effective research."

On the other hand, people who answered no to question 10 felt that, even given instruction, students do not bother to use content from the Invisible Web. A certain defeatist attitude regarding students' unwillingness to include database content in their research tends to seep through these answers:

- "No, because they cannot be bothered to use [the Invisible Web]."
- "I have not had anyone tell me that they have used it for research."
- "Struggling students find our databases difficult to read and understand."
- "No, not really. I think searching the Invisible Web is a bit difficult with minimal return."
- "It depends on how open they are to learning something new about the web when they think they already know everything they need to know about it and how willing they are to spend the time searching the web deeply. Many just want to find something quickly and get their paper done."
- "Yes, if they are actually motivated and not just completing a class requirement."
- "Depends on their motivation."

FIGURE 3.9 Do you think that learning about the Invisible Web helps students with their research? (*n* = 390)

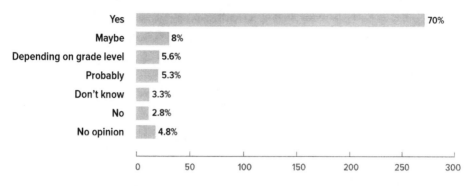

Source: Invisible Web/Deep Web/Hidden Web survey, question 10 (see appendix).

However, it must be pointed out that only 390 people answered this question while 631 skipped it. Respondents were again self-selected, limited to those who had a specific motivation to answer the question (or, in some cases perhaps, to air a grievance).

The question of educational levels came up again: some answered no to question 10 because they felt that teaching the Invisible Web was inappropriate for a certain level, while others answered yes, but only at a particular level. Those who answered "yes, but" and specified the level—anywhere from high school to graduate students—are counted in the category "Depending on grade level" in figure 3.9 (*n* = 22, 5.6%). More detailed information on the question of educational levels can be found in the responses to question 11. Another recurring theme is the issue of need. Students will learn if they feel a compelling need; instruction about sources that make up the Invisible Web is more effective when it is introduced to students who are facing a deadline for a research paper.

Question 11: Should every student be taught about the Invisible Web, and if so, at what grade level?

The greatest discrepancy among responses to the survey questions had to do with the appropriate level at which to introduce the Invisible Web. Respondents included public, school, and academic librarians and educators, and there seems to be no consensus on this point. Answers about when to teach ran the gamut from K–6 to PhD level. One respondent argued that the Invisible Web should be taught during an entire week in the ninth grade.

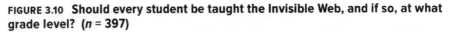

FIGURE 3.10 **Should every student be taught the Invisible Web, and if so, at what grade level?** (*n* = 397)

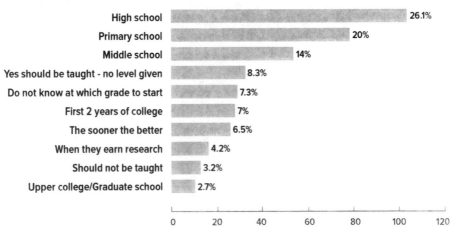

Source: Invisible Web/Deep Web/Hidden Web survey, question 11 (see appendix).

Others argued for teaching it to high school seniors. Some felt strongly that the Invisible Web should be taught only in advanced research classes at upper levels, such as the master's or PhD level. Community colleges were singled out three times: One respondent felt that community college students "do not have the contextual knowledge necessary to know where to 'place' information." Another suggested that they "have a hard enough time getting through web basics and library database information." And yet another respondent had the exact opposite interpretation that, on the contrary, community college students "should know that not all information available on the Internet is accessible, but that it exists."

The most prevalent response as to when to teach about the Invisible Web was high school (*n* = 104, 26.1%; see fig. 3.10). This group thought that high school students were doing research assignments and would benefit from the instruction. There were also strong opinions (20%) about teaching some aspects of the Invisible Web in primary schools. Those responders felt that students should start their research life with a better basis than just using Google. Combining the 20% who voted for primary schools with those who thought "the sooner the better" (6.5%) or "when they learn to research" (4.2%), it would seem that primary school may be the preferred level to begin teaching the Invisible Web.

A few people commented on the fact that it is not only students who should be taught about the Invisible Web but teachers too. One graduate student wrote that she was completing her first year in an accredited MLIS program and had never heard of the Invisible Web.

Question 12: If you have any additional comments, please share them here. This section of the survey simply asked if anyone had any additional comments. A number of people expressed their interest and encouragement for the project and survey topic. Some respondents, especially those who did not know about the Invisible Web, expressed their frustration with the survey. We appreciated the feedback, favorable or not.

Some people took the opportunity to express more about their view of the Invisible Web and teaching. Here are a few samples of these responses, both positive and negative:

- "I consider some of the pre-occupation with the deep web is over-kill. It's there—individuals need to be aware of it—it may be useful—but it is only a part of the whole picture."
- "My experience has been that the student needs to see immediate results. They also need to have the presentation of the invisible web tied to their own immediate interests. The demonstration/ instruction needs to yield results relevant to their research."
- "I would like more time and guidance to learn about the Invisible Web before I had the confidence to teach it myself."
- "Teaching these skills successfully can only be achieved as part of a scaffolded and integrated approach to information literacy education."
- "The thing I find the hardest about teaching anything web/ online-related is the 'oh, computers; I know all about computers' when my students at best have shallow searching experience. 'Invisible' sites and resources can help, especially when it's time to go from 'you can use these exact sites' to 'how do you find quality material that is worth using in assignments.'"
- "Maybe one reason it's hard to get kids beyond Google is that they don't know what they don't know!"

Analysis of Part Two of the Survey

- Most people (78%) do think that the Invisible Web should be taught.
- A majority (70%) agree that it would help students with their research.
- There were advocates for teaching the Invisible Web on all grade levels. Those who responded that it should be taught in primary schools think that the Invisible Web should be included in introductions to the web and to the concept of searching for information. The middle school supporters think that discussions about research begin during those years. High school advocates think that it would help students doing research assignments. These are all good reasons and suggest that staged learning at all these grade levels would benefit all. Those who suggested college as the appropriate place for introducing the Invisible Web see it as a function of advanced searching skills.
- People suggested various ways to introduce the Invisible Web to students, mostly not as a separate lesson but as part of discussions of search engines and in conjunction with assignments.
- More than half of the respondents answered that they do *not* teach about the Invisible Web at any grade level. Throughout the survey, there was a persistent minority that did not think that the Invisible Web should be taught. That group needs to be persuaded as to its value. For those already convinced, there needs to be more help to make it easier to introduce the Invisible Web into teaching.
- What comes through loud and clear is that those who know about the Invisible Web because they have used it in their own research find it easier to teach about it or, at least, to refer to it in conjunction with class presentations.
- Time was a factor often mentioned. Six people ($n = 6$, 1%) felt strongly about the need to teach the Invisible Web but lamented the lack of time in students' already overburdened schedules. They claimed that it was practically impossible to add anything to their classes or presentations.

CONCLUSION

What does our survey say about how the concept of the Invisible Web resonates with teaching faculty and librarians? About two-thirds of respondents (64%) knew of the Invisible Web (question 1), and 56% were one step ahead in that they have used it in their own research (question 4). Of course, anyone who has ever conducted research by looking for sources in a subscription database has used the Invisible Web. The question that remains is \why 8% have not used the Invisible Web even though they claimed to know about it.

As for teaching, 43.4% answered that they have actually taught the Invisible Web in some form or another (question 6). Why is there a difference between those who know about the Invisible Web (64%) and those who teach about it (43.4%)? Why is it not more valued in today's Googlized world to impart this knowledge to users? One reason that was mentioned by a few respondents and touched on above is time: today's K–12 curricula are so packed that it is indeed very hard to incorporate one more concept into the teaching load. Another reason may be that Invisible Web sources are, in fact, used but not identified as such. Even faculty who teach about the complexities of research may not refer to it by name. Librarians, too, often help students at the reference desk to find articles in subscription databases without stopping to mention the duality of search engines versus databases or free versus fee-based sources. We would argue, however, that in today's digitized world using the correct nomenclature is all the more critical, as students' research is becoming more and more one-sided. As we have seen, for many students, "Google is the Internet" (quoted in Hatch 2011, 958). This is not to say that Google is not a valid research tool, but it should not be the only one. In every class, at every reference desk, or at any other pedagogical opportunity, educators in every discipline should at a minimum encourage discussion about search engines versus databases, the two information sources most used to introduce the Invisible Web in teaching (question 9).

It is becoming evident that anyone involved with students conducting research, no matter what the educational level, must be familiar with students' information-seeking behaviors. These were explored in chapter 2:

access trumps content, saving time is primary, and Google reigns supreme. Respondents alluded to these traits in answers to several questions in the survey. But they did not necessarily view teaching about the Invisible Web as a way to mitigate the weaknesses of student research. The Invisible Web as a concept did not seem to translate seamlessly into use or into teaching.

But the concept of the Invisible Web as it intersects with research is an important one, and it is best raised in school at a very early age. At what level? High school was the level most mentioned, followed by primary or elementary school, middle school, and college. The consensus seemed to be that the earlier educators start introducing the various research sources the better prepared students will be once they reach college. The same logic applies in public libraries or any other educational situation: the earlier users confront all the various sources available for research, the better prepared they will be for everyday life research. What emerges from our survey is that educators need to know about the Invisible Web, use it themselves, and then teach it to their students, because the data show that such instruction is not being consistently implemented.

One person took the trouble to write the following: "I have had students report back from college that they have used it in class and their professors have asked them to show them how they got their results because they were surprised they were so thorough and complete." A goal that all educators should aim for.

REFERENCES

Boswell, Wendy. 2007. *The About.com Guide to Online Research: Navigate the Web—from RSS and the Invisible Web to Multimedia and the Blogosphere.* About.com Guides. Avon, MA: Adams Media.

Diaz, Karen R. 2000. "The Invisible Web: Navigating the Web outside Traditional Search Engines." *Reference & User Services Quarterly* 40, no. 2: 131–134. Academic Search Complete.

Hatch, David. 2011. "Google's Dominance: Is the Online-Search Giant Too Powerful?" *CQ Researcher* 21, no. 40: 953–976.

Henninger, Maureen. 2008. *The Hidden Web: Finding Quality Information on the Net.* 2nd ed. Sydney: UNSW Press.

Ru, Yanbo, and Ellis Horowitz. 2005. "Indexing the Invisible Web: A Survey." *Online Information Review* 29, no. 3: 249–265. http://dx.doi org/10.1108/14684520510607579.

HOW TO MAKE STUDENTS BETTER RESEARCHERS: THE INVISIBLE WEB IN TEACHING

A S HAS BEEN SEEN IN THE PREVIOUS CHAP-ters, the research process is a tortuous affair for most students. The single and national studies analyzed in chapter 2 highlighted the problems of too much information and the difficulty of navigating databases, which make up more than half of the Invisible Web (Bergman 2001), compared to the ease of using Google and related issues of time. The results of our survey, presented in chapter 3, reinforced the prevalence of some of these difficulties that students encounter when conducting research.

The premise of this book is that a knowledge of the Invisible Web can help make students better researchers. Why does the Invisible Web have this power? To begin with, the Invisible Web is a metaphor for better searching, as it encompasses a myriad of valuable sources found primarily in databases. It thus offers all users a bigger toolbox, with more potential and more room to explore. This larger toolbox might sound counterproductive when one of the biggest complaints students have is that they feel over-whelmed by the abundance of materials available on the web. Indeed, the move from relying entirely on Google to using general and eventually more specialized databases does, at first, seem to represent an unwelcome increase in complexity. But as students become more comfortable with these databases, the pool of search tools from which they work will shrink as they begin to master the ability to zero in on a smaller number of sources related to their topic. As students progress from their early education through college to finally establish themselves in a career, they can grow more sophisticated in their approach to research as their knowledge about searching not only the Invisible Web but also the surface web increases.

Information overload is so pervasive today that students are turning to known entities for help. According to the research analyzed in chapter 2, these resources do not include librarians. Students instead fall back on their immediate environment, which as always includes friends and family but now also includes an added dimension, social networking sites.

This chapter will look at certain critical issues of information-seeking behavior interlaced with a series of scenarios on how to make students better researchers using Invisible Web content. Some of these scenarios have been gleaned from our survey (chapter 3); others, from experts and colleagues in the information field who have graciously agreed to share their strategies with us. The word *student* in this chapter refers primarily to practitioners of academic research, but the principles discussed here apply equally to any web user conducting research, whether of an academic nature or for everyday life.

DIFFICULTIES WITH RESEARCH

THE INFORMATION-SEEKING ROLLER COASTER

It is common knowledge that research is hard work. This is especially true in today's fast-paced, information-driven society, where, at the click of a mouse, millions of answers are readily available to anyone. Students naturally feel quickly overwhelmed. Gary Price, coauthor of the groundbreaking work on the Invisible Web (Sherman and Price 2001), once said that everything beyond the first page of results in a search engine can be considered part of the Invisible Web (Notess 2006, 167)! Before delving into the various issues that contribute to this research-related anxiety, a selective review of learning theory as it pertains to information-seeking behavior is warranted.

The beginning of the research process is characterized by an unease with the overwhelming amount of information, a lack of evaluation skills, and a pressing sense of time. Head and Eisenberg, in a 2010 Project Information Literacy Progress Report, surveyed 8,353 college students on twenty-five campuses in the spring of 2010 and identified the areas in which students encountered difficulties in the research process. As part of their study, they asked students twenty questions related to the various steps involved in conducting course-related research, many of which were tied to using Invisible Web content. Students rated the statements along a scale (strongly agree, somewhat agree, neither agree or disagree, somewhat disagree, strongly disagree) (Head and Eisenberg 2010, 24). The results suggest that the four most difficult steps during the course-related research process are getting started (84% of students reported this), defining a topic (66%), narrowing it down (62%), and filtering irrelevant results (61%) (see fig. 4.1).

FIGURE 4.1 Difficulties with the research process

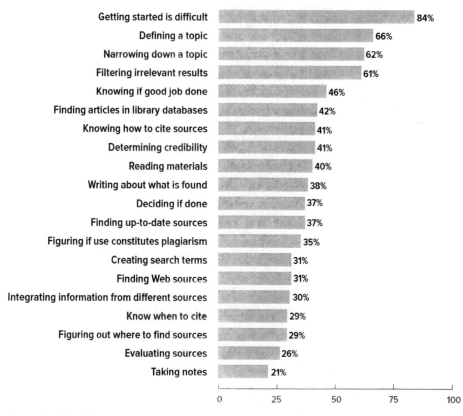

Source: *Truth Be Told: How College Students Evaluate and Use Information in the Digital Age* (Head and Eisenberg 2010, 25).

Filtering irrelevant results is apparently rendered more difficult by using the web to find sources. Only 42% of students reported "finding articles in library databases" as difficult, a significantly lower percentage than for filtering irrelevant results. Using articles from subscription databases that students have access to makes the evaluation process that much easier. A similar set of questions from the same survey asked students to evaluate everyday life research. This time, filtering irrelevant results was rated as the most difficult task (41%) (Head and Eisenberg 2010, 27). In an earlier report, Head and Eisenberg (2009) had already outlined the frustrations and challenges that confront today's students when conducting research. This study involved group discussions with students on seven U.S. campuses in the fall of 2008. For course-related research, the top three complaints that students identified, listed from most to least frequently, were

- information overload;
- too much irrelevant information; and
- beginning and getting started on an assignment (Head and Eisenberg 2009, 4).

The frustrations and challenges listed above resonate with Carol Kuhlthau's work on the information search process. Kuhlthau divides the research process into seven sequential stages, each with three sets of characteristics: namely, affective (feelings), cognitive (thoughts), and physical (actions) (Kuhlthau 2004, 99). The first six stages are as follows:

- Initiation—to recognize an information need
- Selection—to identify a general topic
- Exploration—to investigate information on the general topic
- Formulation—to formulate a focus
- Collection—to gather information pertaining to the focus
- Presentation—to complete the information search

(The seventh, assessment, is beyond the scope of this analysis.) Kuhlthau depicts these six stages on a continuum (see fig. 4.2).

The first stage, "initiation," is characterized chiefly by uncertainty. Kuhlthau defines uncertainty as "a cognitive state that commonly causes affective symptoms of anxiety and lack of confidence" (Kuhlthau 2004, 92). These feelings of "uncertainty, confusion and frustration," coupled with a

FIGURE 4.2 **Model of the information search process**

	Initiation	Selection	Exploration	Formulation	Collection	Presentation	Assessment
Feelings (Affective)	Uncertainty	Optimism	Confusion Frustration Doubt	Clarity	Sense of direction/ Confidence	Satisfaction or Disappointment	Sense of accomplishment
Thoughts (Cognitive)	vague —————————————————→ focused ————————————————————→ increased interest						Increased self-awareness
Actions (Physical)	seeking relevant information Exploring ————————→				seeking pertinent information Documenting ————————→		

Source: *Seeking Meaning: A Process Approach to Library and Information Services*, 2nd ed. (Kuhlthau 2004, 82).

lack of confidence, are present at the beginning, when a student receives an assignment and has no idea how to tackle the topic or where to begin (Head and Eisenberg 2010; Kuhlthau 2004). Such feelings are heightened if a student is familiar only with the surface web. A student aware of sources available through the Invisible Web can move faster from this uncertain "initiation" stage to the second stage, "selection" (identifying a general topic). At this juncture, most students rely heavily on Wikipedia to obtain an overall view of a topic. Wikipedia is, of course, a visible website of uncertain reliability. By now, students have generally been taught to double-check all facts and ideas they find in Wikipedia, as they know that entries can be contributed and edited by anyone. However, they often do not know about Invisible Web sources for similar information. More authoritative online encyclopedias are published within specific disciplines, and these can provide more scholarly topic overviews. Such sources, often part of the Invisible Web, promote a certain peace of mind that comes from using sources written and vetted by experts.

Having chosen a broad topic, the student is faced with the third task, "exploration." With this stage, the student's feelings turn from momentary optimism to confusion, frustration, and doubt—a normal corollary of topic investigation. If students can be gradually steered toward appropriate, specialized databases that focus their searches and decrease the number of relevant results, their level of anxiety will go down while their confidence rises. Left to their own devices at this stage, students often turn their research over to Google, regardless of its well-known pitfalls (see chapter 2). Intervention by educators is necessary at this exploratory stage and again at the later stage of "collection," after a topic has been formulated. This intervention can take the form of guidance in the choice and use of databases to produce a smaller, more targeted number of results. The overall idea behind this theory is to move students from uncertainty to understanding (Kuhlthau 2004, 105), a process rendered easier when they rely more on Invisible Web content than simply on sources from general-purpose search engines.

Some faculty steer students toward specific links which they have selected in advance. Although this helps students complete the research assignment, it takes away their agency when it comes to selection, use, and evaluation of materials. It ultimately does not help students with the research process or with the process of developing critical thinking skills. Giving students the tools they need to find their own way, on the other hand, will not only alleviate the pain during the beginning stages of research but also instill better research habits.

Traditionally, in the first year or two of college, students receive library instruction when they need sources to write a research paper, usually in a beginning English class. A variety of reference services have been in place in libraries for a very long time. Newer services are always being implemented and one, called advisory reference, gives a student the opportunity to make a one-on-one appointment with a librarian. During this meeting, a librarian will typically work with the student on the topic at hand and steer the student toward specialized databases that the library subscribes to. Another common service is the embedded librarian, who is assigned to a particular class and can thus work with students throughout the entire research process, offering guidance in the selection and use of databases geared toward the topics of a particular class assignment. The embedded librarian usually works in the online environment (Matthew and Schroeder 2006), but he or she can also work in a face-to-face class. It is a collaboration between faculty and librarian which allows students to receive help at a much earlier stage, when the research process is first explained. During all of these various encounters, librarians stress use of subscription databases as a way to alleviate students' feelings of anxiety and frustration with research.

As we have seen, Head and Eisenberg identify getting started with a research project as the most difficult step (fig. 4.1). And Kuhlthau characterizes this step by students' uncertain feelings and vague thoughts (fig. 4.2). When turning to the process of selecting materials, students gain a sense of optimism, followed again by confusion, frustration, and doubt as they face an overabundance of material. It therefore behooves educators, faculty, and librarians to intervene very early on to offer support. Kuhlthau calls these opportunities "zones of intervention" (Kuhlthau 2004, 128–129). Faculty and librarians need to become sensitive to the ebb and flow of feelings associated with the various steps of the research process and be ready to address it with students. By placing more emphasis on the various affective stages within the research process and rooting the concept of the Invisible Web within the first few stages, faculty help lessen what is often for students a terrible sense of confusion and frustration. Working with students to define, broaden, or narrow their topics by showing them a variety of general sources from the surface web as well as introducing them to the Invisible Web will alleviate their sense of uncertainty throughout the roller coaster ride that is academic research.

OVERABUNDANCE OF MATERIAL

Studies analyzed in chapter 2 revealed that one of the causes of poor research is the overwhelming number of sources students find when using only general-purpose search engines (Hampton-Reeves et al. 2009; Head and Eisenberg 2010). Not only do students tend to stick primarily to the surface web when conducting research, but they also get buried under hundreds of results, unable to find their way out of the plethora of web pages, documents, videos, images, blog postings, and more, yielded by their visible web searches. Their task is truly akin to finding a needle in a haystack! The results of the survey analyzed in chapter 3 reiterated this theme: respondents to question 7 (Do you think students should be taught about the Invisible Web?) noted that students need to learn about Invisible Web content to counteract the overabundance of information they find through Google, a dilemma that often has the effect of paralyzing student efforts.

One solution to this overabundance of material is to introduce students to databases, which make up the bulk of the Invisible Web. A good researcher has to use more than one tool: search engines, yes, but also web directories, subscription databases, library catalogs, and others. The process we are advocating will initially take more time—nor will it immediately resolve the issue of information overload. However, as students become familiar with using more targeted and vetted search tools, they will retrieve better resources and save time. The validity of this point can be demonstrated in class by means of a compare and contrast exercise. Many respondents to question 9 of our survey (How do you introduce the Invisible Web when teaching?) mentioned this technique:

- "I demo a search using Google and show the hits, then I demo the same search term using a database, or even just adding 'database' to the search term in Google."
- "When students are doing their thesis papers, we talk about the difference between websites vs. databases. That is when I mention the Invisible Web."
- "I introduce the invisible web by comparing search results using search engines, subject directories and databases."
- "Model a query with unsatisfactory results in a common search engine, then introduce the same query in a deep resource (statistics are good for this!)."

An example of a comparison exercise follows, using the search phrase "Invisible Web." A January 2012 Google search for the phrase "Invisible Web" pulled up 872,000 results, the first ten of which appear in figure 4.3.

FIGURE 4.3 **First ten results of a Google search for "Invisible Web"**

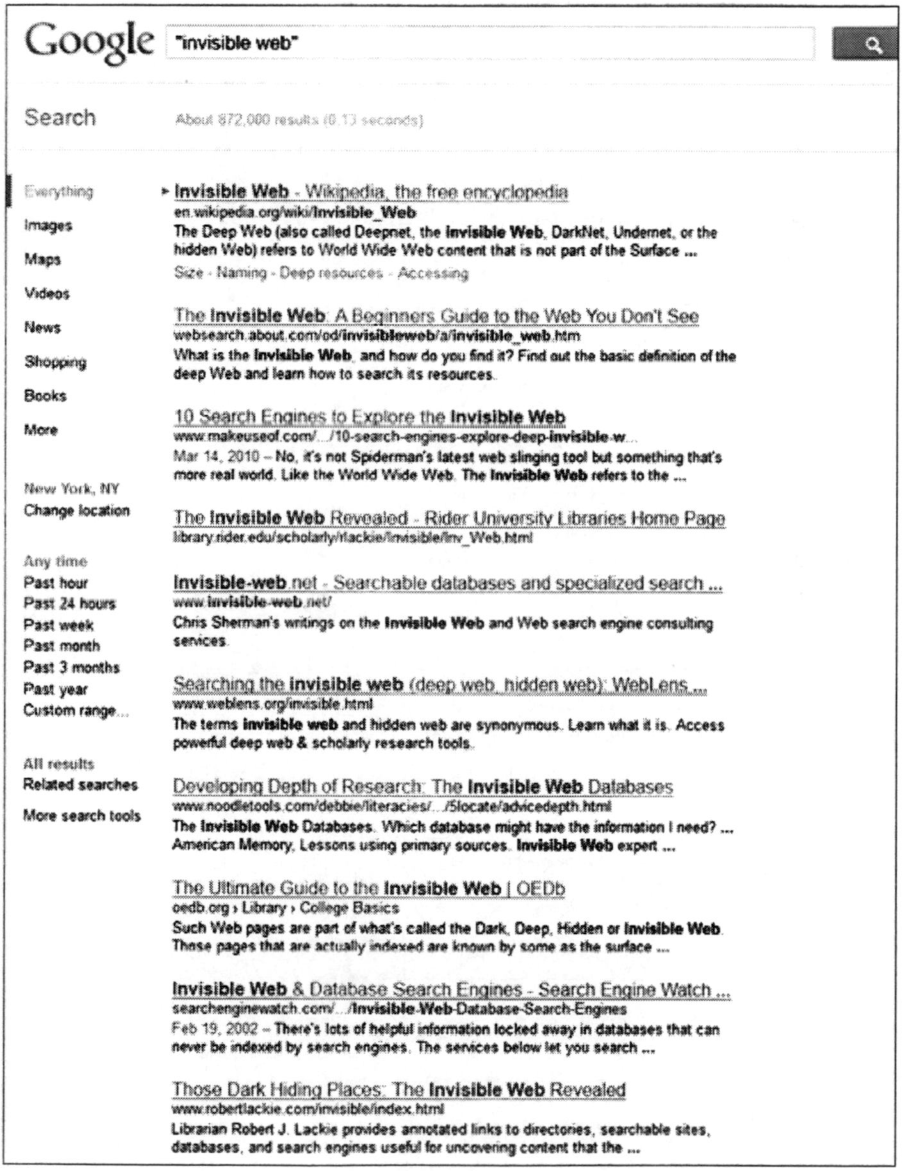

The same search conducted in a full-text library database, Library Literature & Information Science Full Text (LLIS), available through EBSCOhost at our institution, LaGuardia Community College/CUNY, pulled up just 54 results (see fig. 4.4 for the first ten). In each keyword search, quotation marks were used around the two words to maintain them as a phrase, and relevance was the default limiter in the subscription database. (This search was undertaken in a database that is no longer extant owing to the acquisition of H. W. Wilson by EBSCO, but the principles of the search remain valid.)

A comparison of the first ten results of these two searches appears in table 4.1.

FIGURE 4.4 **First ten results of a search for "Invisible Web" in Library Literature & Information Science Full Text**

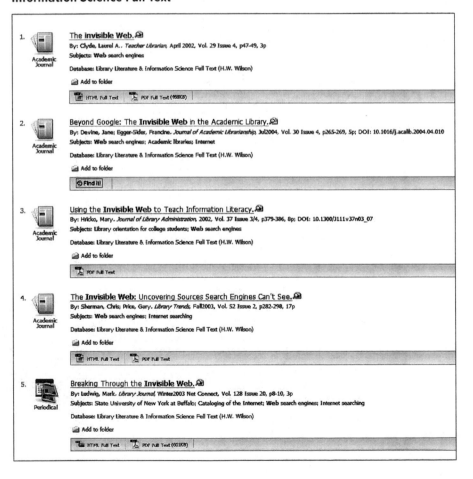

FIGURE 4.4 (continued)

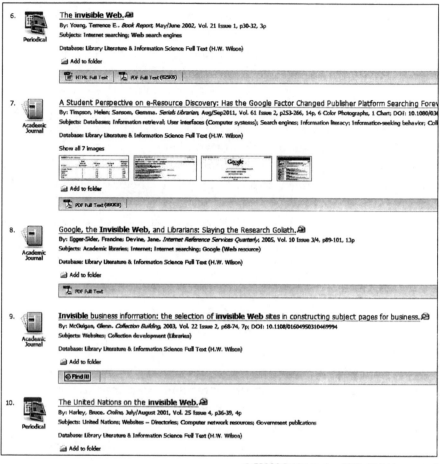

An analysis and comparison of the results of these two searches is instructive. The first element to consider is the number of results found: as we've already seen, the Google search produced 872,000 results, compared to 54 for LLIS. A student doing research on the topic of the Invisible Web could easily browse through the titles of 54 results. It is impossible to do that with 872,000 results. As we saw in chapter 2, students usually do not look beyond the first page of results, creating another layer of invisibility for the searches in both interfaces.

Another element of comparison is type of source. The first ten results found through Google include two blog posts, one online encyclopedia entry (in Wikipedia, naturally), two websites (one of them under construction), and five website articles, two of which are duplicates. By comparison, the initial ten results for the same search in LLIS yielded seven scholarly journal articles and three magazine articles; five of the seven journal articles and all three magazine articles are full text.

It might be useful to compare other elements of these search results using a guide or checklist for the evaluation of electronic resources. One such guide is Robert Harris's CARS Checklist for Information Quality (Harris 2010), which presents a straightforward approach to evaluation of web sources and offers students an easy mnemonic: CARS stands for **C**redibility, **A**ccuracy, **R**easonableness, and **S**upport. For the first criterion of value, credibility, the author's credentials are crucial. Verifying the identities of the authors of the articles in the LLIS results list was no more complicated than following the byline to the statement of the authors' credentials (typically either on the first page or at the end of an article). In this case, all the authors have a professional link in the field of education, primarily in libraries: they are either professors or librarians (or both) in colleges and universities, thus providing a context within which they wrote about the Invisible Web. Chris Sherman and Gary Price (table 4.1, source L4) are the authors of the first book on the Invisible Web, titled *The Invisible Web: Uncovering Sources Search Engines Can't See* and published in 2001. Timpson and Sansom (L7) were Library and Information Science students in London when they wrote their 2011 article comparing the use of Google Scholar versus proprietary subject databases.

By contrast, verifying who was behind some of the websites that Google ranked in the first ten spots of its results list proved to be much harder. It took detective work and many searches—for which Google proved to be an excellent general-purpose search engine—to find out anything about the Online Education Database (OEDb, source G8). OEDb, which rates online programs at accredited colleges and universities, is a private, for-profit company started in 2006. However, this latter information is provided in a *Chronicle of Higher Education* article (Kolowich 2009) as well as various blog postings but not on the website itself; the lack of transparency damages the website's credibility. Similarly, it took time to discover that Weblens.org (source G6) is a site maintained by Pam Blackstone, who is a photojournalist and a designer. Her site, dated 2005, no longer meets the standards for currency.

TABLE 4.1

Comparison of search for "Invisible Web" using Google and Library Literature & Information Science Full Text (January 2012)

Google	Library Literature & Information Science (LLIS)
G1. [Encyclopedia entry] **Invisible Web—** Wikipedia, the free encyclopedia	**L1.** [Journal article] **The Invisible Web—**By Laurel A. Clyde, professor at the University of Iceland, Reykjavik, in *Teacher Librarian,* 2002
G2. [Website article] **The Invisible Web: A Beginners Guide to the Web You Don't See**—About.com, a *New York Times* website; article by Wendy Boswell, IW expert; article undated (site date 2011)	**L2.** [Journal article] **Beyond Google: The Invisible Web in the Academic Library**—By Devine and Egger-Sider, published in the *Journal of Academic Librarianship,* 2004
G3. [Blog post] **10 Search Engines to Explore the Invisible Web**—By Saikat Basu, staff author for MakeUseOf, a blog about the web; posted on March 10, 2010	**L3.** [Journal article] **Using the Invisible Web to Teach Information Literacy**—By Mary Hricko, library director, Kent State University, Geauga Campus, in the *Journal of Library Administration,* 2003; not full text
G4. [Website article] **The Invisible Web Revealed—Libraries—Rider University**—A well-known website/article on the IW created by Robert J. Lackie, professor at Rider University, NJ, in May 2001; last updated May 2009	**L4.** [Journal article] **The Invisible Web: Uncovering Sources Search Engines Can't See**—By Sherman and Price (authors of first book on the Invisible Web), in *Library Trends,* 2003; a partial excerpt of their book by the same title
G5. [Website] **Invisible-Web.net—Searchable databases and specialized search** . . . —Marketed as companion website to seminal work on the IW by Sherman & Price but remains under construction	**L5.** [Magazine article] **Breaking Through the Invisible Web**—Feature article by Mark Ludwig, manager of library systems at SUNY Buffalo, in *Library Journal,* 2003
G6. [Website] **Searching the Invisible Web (Deep Web, Hidden Web); WebLens**— Net search site provided by Pam Blackstone; last updated 2005	**L6.** [Magazine article] **The Invisible Web**—By Terrence E. Young, school library media specialist in New Orleans, LA, and adjunct instructor in library science at the University of New Orleans, in *Book Report,* 2002; geared toward school media specialists
G7. [Website article] **Developing Depth of Research: The Invisible Web Databases**—NoodleTools, founded by Debbie and Damon Abilock; list of IW databases; several links broken; no date provided; targeted to high school students and teachers	**L7.** [Journal article] **A Student Perspective on e-Resource Discovery: Has the Google Factor Changed Publisher Platform Searching Forever?**—By Timpson and Sansom, LIS students at City University London, in *Serials Librarian,* 2011; not full text

(Continued on page 100)

G8. [Website article] **The Ultimate Guide to the Invisible Web OEDb**—Online Education Database (private company), founded in 2006; reviews accredited online colleges and universities; last updated December 2006

G9. [Blog post] **Invisible Web & Database Search Engines—Search Engine Watch**—Very short entry by Danny Sullivan, founding editor of *Search Engine Watch*; dated February 19, 2002; not updated

G10. [Website article] **Those Dark Hiding Places: The Invisible Web Revealed**— The direct link to this website on the IW by Robert J. Lackie also listed above (G4); dated May 29, 2001

L8. [Journal article] **Google, the Invisible Web, and Librarians: Slaying the Research Goliath**—By Egger-Sider and Devine, in *Internet Reference Services Quarterly*, 2005

L9. [Journal article] **Invisible Business Information: The Selection of IW Sites in Constructing Subject Pages for Business**—By Glenn McGuigan, business and public administration reference librarian at Penn State, Harrisburg, in *Collection Building*, 2003; not full text

L10. [Journal article] **The United Nations on the Invisible Web**—By Bruce Harley, reference librarian at San Diego State University, in *Online*, 2001

The credibility of other items in the Google results list varies considerably. In source G3, the author of the blog post, Saikat Basu, does not seem ever to have written on the Invisible Web in the past. He works in the technology field but does not have a track record regarding the Invisible Web. The NoodleTools website (source G7) is a mother-and-son venture operated since 1999 by Debbie and Damon Abilock: according to information on the site at the time of our search, Debbie has over twenty-five years of experience in education while Damon's expertise is in computer science and user interface design. NoodleTools includes a page on Invisible Web databases geared toward high school students. The entry from Wikipedia (source G1), the free encyclopedia that anyone can edit, reveals a poorly written and researched article followed by an incomplete bibliography. Wendy Boswell (source G2) has been, for many years, a guide to web search on the About.com site, which is owned by the *New York Times*. Boswell is a well-established expert on web searching and has published a book on the topic, *The About.com Guide to Online Research: Navigate the Web—from RSS and the Invisible Web to Multimedia and the Blogosphere*. Danny Sullivan, a founding editor of the well-known site *Search Engine Watch*, is the author of the blog post listed as source G9. In this case, although the author is extremely well-respected in technology circles, the particular post is extremely brief and does not provide any valuable information regarding the Invisible Web.

It is clear, at least from this exercise of checking into the credibility of search results, that the ease of verification of author credentials in sources found through a database like LLIS is an excellent reason to conduct research in the Invisible Web. A lack of transparency about author credentials, more common in visible web sources, is a powerful indicator of lack of value in materials found through Google and other general-purpose search engines.

Regarding the second category in the CARS checklist, accuracy, one website listed in table 4.1 (source G5) simply does not work, another (G7) suffers from broken links, and several more (G3, G4, G6, G7, G8, G9, and G10) are out-of-date. The nonfunctioning website, Invisible-Web.net, was marketed by Sherman and Price as a companion to their book on the Invisible Web. However, this website never really materialized: it has been labeled "under construction" or "being refurbished" since its inception, but it is still picked up by crawlers searching for "Invisible Web." The article on the Invisible Web written by Wendy Boswell (G2) on About.com may be up-to-date, but it is difficult to determine this: the site lists no publication date for the article (the site itself carries an up-to-date copyright date, which is not necessarily the same thing). The entry in Wikipedia (G1) fails the test of accuracy for the topic of Invisible Web. Source G4, "The Invisible Web Revealed," is actually the same item as source G10, "Those Dark Hiding Places: The Invisible Web Revealed." Source G4, now out of date, redirects the user to the website by Robert J. Lackie, a professor-librarian at Rider University in Lawrenceville, New Jersey. From there, you get a link to the final version of the article alongside a warning that the site is no longer being updated (as of May 2009).

The same criticism regarding timeliness can be leveled at all the articles found through LLIS, but formally published articles, whether in journals or in magazines, represent, by their nature, a slice in time when they are written. If they were accurate at the time of writing, they remain valuable for the researcher. Websites are inherently fluid entities which can—and should—be updated on a regular basis. From that standpoint, the criterion of accuracy is more stringent for websites than for periodical literature, especially for a quickly evolving topic such as the Invisible Web.

The category of reasonableness, which includes fairness, balance, and objectivity, does not seem to apply to a complex but, on the whole, uncontroversial topic. Nonetheless, as the OEDb example (G8) illustrates, it is important to be aware of the potential for commercial interests in favor of, for example, one particular institution or database over another.

In terms of support, the final CARS criterion, the articles found in LLIS all provide sources related to the Invisible Web, whether in the article itself or as part of a bibliography at the end. The same can be said for all the website sources found through Google except for the one that remains under construction (G5). The journal articles, however, tend to offer lengthier, more scholarly bibliographies than the website sources. Interestingly, the reference lists in several of the LLIS articles contain links to several of the sources pulled up by the Google search.

The topic chosen for this compare-and-contrast exercise is academic by nature. If a different search had been chosen, for "teenage pregnancy" or "solar energy," for example, the differences between the results found using Google versus a subscription database would have been even more obvious. With a more academic topic, the differences are more nuanced and thus harder to evaluate. It is far easier for students to identify glaringly commercial sites or websites with obvious political or other biases—and omit them accordingly. Nonetheless, a compare-and-contrast exercise such as the one undertaken here can be done on a much smaller scale at various grade levels and still highlight the fact that to write a complete paper on the topic of the Invisible Web, students will need results from both visible web and Invisible Web sources.

THE PITFALLS OF EVALUATION

A compare-and-contrast exercise ultimately leads to a discussion of the validity and authority of sources, as demonstrated in the previous section. Invisible Web content is, by its nature, already vetted, as editors of databases make decisions as to what to include. Human intervention takes place for each article chosen, whereas search engines work as automated crawlers picking up link after link on the web. In a Google search, students tend to work only with results on the first page and to equate relevance with authority. They trust Google's PageRank algorithm to put the results in descending order of relevance for their own research paper. Students perceive themselves as good at evaluation (see table 2.5), when in fact they have great difficulty with the evaluation of web sources.

One of the biggest hurdles for students in the evaluation of web sources is determining the type of document and format their searches pull up: Is the item a website (and if so, who publishes it)? Is it a web page that is part of a larger website? Is it a blog post (as source G3 in table 4.1)? A government document? An article published by a content farm? (A *content farm* is defined by the news and technology blog *Mashable* as "a company that employs large numbers of often freelance writers to generate large amounts of textual content which is specifically designed to satisfy algorithms for maximum retrieval by automated search engines"; http://mashable.com/follow/topics/content-farms/.) Students can easily stumble upon any of these various source types when searching the surface web. But when is a blog article or other website content a good source for a research paper? Google announced on February 24, 2011 (well before we did our compare-and-contrast exercise), that it had introduced "a pretty big algorithmic improvement" to the way it ranks results, one that "will provide better rankings for high-quality sites—sites with original content and information such as research, in-depth reports, thoughtful analysis and so on" (Singhal and Cutts 2011). Perhaps. But it takes an analysis like the report by Danny Sullivan on *Search Engine Land*, a news and information site dealing with searching that Sullivan founded after leaving *Search Engine Watch*, to begin to make sense of this apparent pushback by Google against content farms (Sullivan 2011). Students often lack this kind of context when they judge the sources they come across, and this is a major reason why they should be steered toward Invisible Web content, where the information tends to be more reliable. A comparison like the one illustrated in table 4.1 can set the stage for a better grasp on how to evaluate each document or article found.

Databases, as opposed to search engines, pick up a more limited range of source types, primarily electronic articles and e-books. It is critical that students understand that sources found through a database have been previously vetted for inclusion in that database. Sticking to Invisible Web content by focusing searches on databases will not make the work of evaluation unnecessary, but it will make it much easier. Knowing that an article from a general or specialized database has been evaluated by the editors of the tool means the item in question does have some merit. The availability and reliability of databases are crucial for the process of research and must be imparted to students in whenever research takes place. Practicing evaluation techniques such as the ones exemplified by the CARS checklist, within each discipline, will also go a long way in alleviating students' sense of being overwhelmed by research.

EASE OF USE MINDSET

Every piece of literature on information-seeking behavior mentions the importance students place on ease of use. If a tool is not as quick and easy to use as the ubiquitous Google search box, students move on. In everyday life situations, we naturally gravitate toward "the principle of least effort" (Wikipedia 2011). This phenomenon is well documented in the context of student research (De Rosa et al. 2010; Du and Evans 2011; Dubicki 2010; Hanson et al. 2010; Judd and Kennedy 2011). The use of Invisible Web content flies in the face of this principle of least effort because a good researcher must take the time to repeat searches in more than one tool, compare and contrast results, modify the search terms if need be, and so on. Indeed, one of the greatest hurdles librarians face in convincing students to use the databases provided by institutional libraries is that these databases are complex to use and each one of them has a different syntax. Timpson and Sansom sum up students' frustrations: "Google seems to have cornered the market for finding information, as it is an easy to use interface that does not require passwords and is freely available. The navigation of the LMS [Library Management System] can be confusing; accessing the invisible Web is at the very least challenging and at worst impossible" (2011, 256).

Research, then, is a complex and time-consuming endeavor. How can this fact be reconciled with students' need to use simple interfaces? One partial solution is federated searching, which, with one search from a library website, can look through several databases at once. At our home institution, LaGuardia Community College/CUNY, federated searching, dubbed "SuperSearch," is available on the library's home page. Sometimes the grouping is by subject; at other times, results are simply grouped according to the criteria deemed important by the institution's library faculty. Federated searching still entails going to a library website, logging in (if off-campus), and navigating one's way to these databases. But this type of easier access must be offset by the fact that students have shown repeated reluctance (see chapter 2) to work within library subscription databases, let alone a cluster of them. A keyword search on "Invisible Web" in the category Education/Library Science (which includes six EBSCOhost databases: ERIC; Library, Information Science & Technology Abstracts with Full Text; Professional Development Collection; Teacher Reference Center; Education Full Text; and Education Research Complete), with relevance as the default modifier, undertaken at LaGuardia Community College/CUNY in July 2013, produced 130 results, the first four of which are shown in figure 4.5.

Below each result is the name of the database the article is from. Federated searching tries to lure students to valuable content in multiple databases by replicating the simple Google search box. Google Scholar might be an

FIGURE 4.5 **First four results of a search for "Invisible Web" in LaGuardia Community College's SuperSearch In Education/Library Science**

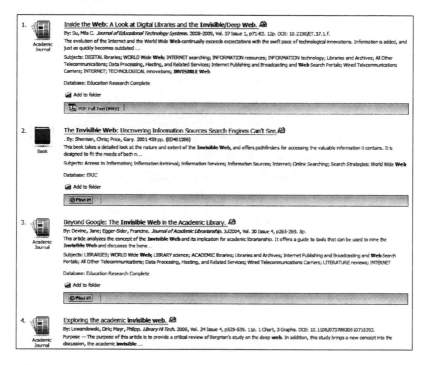

effective compromise. It offers an easy-to-use interface similar to standard Google, and it brings students into contact with academic material, especially if used in conjunction with a library that has full-text linking in place; full-text linking is a mechanism by which users are connected to the full text of an article through a link resolver. Figure 4.6 shows the first six results of a search for the phrase "Invisible Web" in Google Scholar. Note that the full text for three of the sources is available to LaGuardia students.

Although Google Scholar appeals to students for its ease of use coupled with the promise of retrieving more scholarly sources, the first item in the results list in figure 4.6 demonstrates the pitfalls of keyword searching and the need for evaluation, no matter what the search engine, database, or type of source might be. The book title, *The Invisible Web: Gender Patterns in Family Relationships,* includes the phrase "Invisible Web" but deals with

FIGURE 4.6 **First six results of a Google Scholar search for "Invisible Web"**

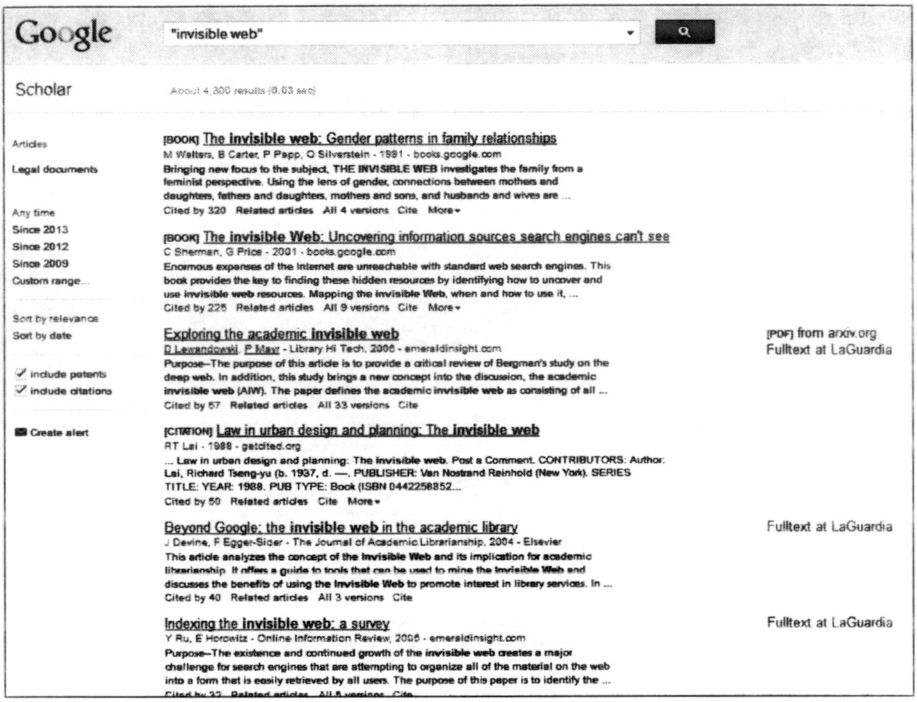

the family from a feminist point of view rather than with the Invisible Web of the information world. The second item in the results list is the Sherman and Price book on the Invisible Web. The third source pulled up through Google Scholar is by Dirk Lewandowski and Philipp Mayr, who have written several articles on the Invisible Web. This article, published in *Library Hi Tech* in 2006, is available through arXiv.org, an open-access archive owned and operated by Cornell University, and thus accessible on the surface web and also through LaGuardia Community College. The fourth source, a book called *Law in Urban Design and Planning: The Invisible Web*, is another example of a keyword search pulling up an item out of context. Thus, in the long run, there is no quick fix to the contradiction between the difficulties of doing research and the principle of least effort, the ease-of-use mindset. In order to become better researchers, students must learn to navigate the various tools at their disposal to come up with the best resources for the topic at hand.

LACK OF TIME

A related issue is time: Time is always of essence, and for students, simply using Google saves time. Today's students are under enormous time constraints, a factor that acts in synergy with the ease-of-use issue addressed above. The Google search box is easy to use and, as a result, students are lured into thinking that a quick search in Google will save time. One can argue, on the contrary, that using a general-purpose search engine and getting lost in a sea of sources will lengthen the time it takes to find the one source that might prove useful. Or, by extension, that a simple search interface like the one used by Google does not necessarily translate into a time savings when it comes to finding sources. In fact, once students become more adept at using Invisible Web content, they will find searching and retrieving valuable sources less time-consuming. Learning how to formulate keyword searches that uncover more focused materials will translate into even less time spent on research. Being precise can actually save time. In addition to saving time, students will avoid the temptation to accept "good enough" results. As students move along in their education, they need to be reminded that research is not a one-stop endeavor.

Research resembles a discovery process in which one link leads to another, one citation leads to another tool, and so forth. To be better researchers, students need to regain a sense of curiosity in this arena. It may be time to entertain the notion of serendipity in the research process as advocated by Nutefall and Ryder (2010), who undertook a survey among instruction librarians and first-year writing faculty and found that serendipity took place in three different "research moments": "chance, mystery investigation, and browsing" (231). A sense of adventure in research can make the entire process more fun, relieve some of the anxiety behind it, and motivate students not to look at the clock so much.

HOW TO TEACH THE INVISIBLE WEB

LEVELS OF INSTRUCTION

From the survey analyzed in chapter 3, it is clear that a great many respondents felt strongly that the concept of the Invisible Web should be taught at an early age in order to instill good research habits in all users. We advocate a staged approach, as students quickly become ingrained in their habits and show a preference for "a limited toolbox of familiar sources" (Head and Eisenberg 2011).

The majority of survey respondents felt that the concept of the Invisible Web is best introduced in high school (chapter 3, fig. 3.10). By then, students have, for the most part, written mainly book reports, although some may have already tackled research. By high school the playing field levels out, in that everyone is asked to conduct research, of literary and other topics. Of course, by the time they enter high school, students have used the web for many years, if for nothing else than social networking sites. They already have a mindset when it comes to using the web.

In fact, the second most common recommendation for introducing the concept of the Invisible Web in teaching was at the primary or elementary level (fig. 3.10). Many recommended including a lesson on the basics of searching as soon as students are introduced to computers. We feel, however, that the concept of the Internet, much less that of the Invisible Web, is too abstract and sophisticated for very young children. That research should be brought into the classroom goes without saying. Indeed, the United States Common Core State Standards Initiative for English Language Arts includes an initiative for research from kindergarten on, under the rubric "Research to Build and Present Knowledge" (www.core standards.org/assets/CCSSI_ELA%20Standards.pdf). The standards get increasingly complex as students progress in years. More advanced concepts can be introduced in the last two years of high school and reiterated for freshmen in college.

CURRICULUM
There is no question that in conducting research, the notion of the Invisible Web will surface. Research assignments, at any level, can and should include a discussion regarding what information is and its provenance—that is, where it comes from. It is up to each teacher to decide what to include and how much to cover. We offered a mix-and-match approach to the learning and teaching of the Invisible Web in research in our first book (Devine and Egger-Sider 2009) and would like to continue within this vein. The topics can be introduced in stages.

Stage One: Web-Searching Basics
Table 4.2 outlines the building blocks which will lead to information literacy skills and set the stage for learning about the Invisible Web.

TABLE 4.2

Stage one concepts: Web-searching basics

A. Search engine basics

1. *Web-searching skills.* These can be basic as needed and more advanced as appropriate.

2. *Realistic expectations for web searching.* Learn what Google is good for and when other tools might be more effective.

3. *How to adapt search phrasing if needed.* Learn to broaden or narrow a search and experiment with different vocabulary.

4. *It is okay to be dissatisfied with search results.* Recognize when results are poor and when to seek better ones.

B. Search tools

1. *Using more than one search tool.* Learn about other search engines, databases, directories, library catalogs, and more.

2. *Subscription databases.* Promote the use of more targeted, vetted materials.

3. *General-purpose search engines.* Promote these as tools, not solutions.

4. *Social networking and social bookmarking sites.* Discuss the use of social media tools for research.

C. Evaluation of information

Depending on students' needs, this can be done simply (e.g., through a review of domains) or more systematically (e.g., using the CARS checklist, www.virtualsalt.com/evalu8it.htm; the Purdue Owl website http://owl.english.purdue.edu/owl/resource/553/1/; or Ithaca College's ICYouSee, www.ithaca.edu/library/training/think.html).

D. Invisible Web vocabulary

An introduction to the Invisible Web through new phrases and expressions.

E. Availability of further help

Where to go for help (librarians, teachers, online reference services, etc.).

Stage Two: Presenting the Invisible Web

Building on the web-searching concepts from stage one, students can now be introduced explicitly to the Invisible Web using the concepts shown in table 4.3.

TABLE 4.3

Stage two concepts: Presenting the Invisible Web

A. Tools and techniques

1. *Compare and contrast.* Execute a search in various search engines, different databases, library catalogs, and more.

2. *Use search engines to find Invisible Web tools.* Add the word "database" to a subject search in Google and it will retrieve Invisible Web resources. Students then need to navigate the database itself.

3. *Other types of sources.* Look for formats that are not well-represented by general-purpose search engines using the tools that can help locate them.

4. *Research vocabulary.* Explore distinctions between databases, directories, catalogs, and so forth.

5. *In-depth and specialized searching.* Teach the use of more specialized research tools—for example, by drilling down into a single subject area.

B. Evaluation of information

1. *Raise expectations.* Students' skills should grow as they progress through their education.

2. *Peer-review and other indicators of authority.* Students should learn to look for content from peer-reviewed journals and other specialized publications.

C. Advanced techniques

1. Assign students to create research journals in which they can explain their research processes and choices.

2. Encourage the use of bookmarks for returning to favorite tools.

3. Remind students frequently of where to seek help with research projects.

D. Using Invisible Web concepts

1. Teach about the size of the Invisible Web compared to the surface web.

2. Teach about the characteristics of Invisible Web resources.

To take one example, as a starting point in an elementary class, a teacher might simply ask students what the word *information* means to them and play with the different answers received. Another approach might entail an overview of search engines. It is important to meet students at their level: if they are going to use Google, why not insert a simple lesson on how Google works? This instruction can be followed by an introduction to an age-appropriate database, such as EBSCOhost's Searchasaurus or Kids Search. Before an assignment is handed out, a high school teacher could introduce the realm of information by deconstructing the web with its search engines and subscription databases, whether students have access to them at school or through a local public library. These many-faceted topics should be revisited and gradually broadened each year until, by high school, students will be familiar with basic search concepts, understand the difference between search engines and databases, and have an idea how to grapple with web evaluation. Starting in college, students will be introduced to more specialized databases while reviewing the various steps involved in the research process and focusing more heavily on the evaluation of sources, whether print or electronic. In an ideal world, these discussions will take place not only in library instruction classes but also within the various disciplines, wherever research is undertaken.

TEACHING ABOUT THE INVISIBLE WEB WITH GRAPHICS

One respondent's answer to question 9 of our survey (How do you introduce the Invisible Web when teaching?) summarizes the importance of graphics in teaching about the Invisible Web: "There are a variety of ways to teach the invisible web . . . But the common thread is showing some kind of visual to help students identify the distinction between what content is considered part of the free web and what content is considered as part of the hidden web." As more than one respondent to the survey suggested, a concise way to depict the place and size of the Invisible Web in the information world is to show an image of an iceberg. The part of the iceberg above water represents the surface or visible web, while the submerged part—which is at least twice the portion above the water—represents the Deep or Invisible Web. Another survey respondent shared that she used a Venn diagram to depict the Invisible Web. These and various other graphics available to capture students' imaginations as to the size of the Invisible Web will be expanded upon in chapter 5.

Another way to convey the size of the Invisible Web is simply to ask students whether they have any idea what percentage of the Internet Google searches. A rough estimate, now dated but still instructive, is the figure of 16%, used by Michael Bergman in the first white paper on the Invisible Web (Bergman 2001). This surprisingly low figure usually stops students in their tracks as they try to wrestle with the implications. Most students—indeed, most users of the web—are under the misconception that a Google search will look at everything available on the web when, in fact, the bulk of the information still resides in the databases that form part of the Invisible Web.

Some students grasp concepts better visually; others learn better by reading an article. A teacher can start by introducing the various metaphors or vocabulary associated with the Invisible Web: icebergs, the ocean, terms like *mining, drilling down, information silos*, and others. There is something for everyone interested in this concept and for every instructor interested in teaching about it. Chapter 5 will offer a selection of tools for visualizing the Invisible Web.

TEACHING ABOUT THE INVISIBLE WEB WITH SOCIAL MEDIA

Students nowadays spend an average of an hour and forty minutes every day on Facebook (Heiberger and Junco 2011). In the 2010 ECAR study cited in chapter 2, 96% of respondents said that they use Facebook, their top two activities being to "stay in touch with friends" (96%) and to "share photos, music, videos, or other work" (72%) (Smith and Caruso 2010, 11). According to the OCLC study *Perceptions of Libraries, 2010*, the proportion of college students using social networking sites is 92% (De Rosa et al. 2010, 60). The real question for our study is whether research forms part of this online sharing. A recent study at Western Michigan University asked its users whether they found Facebook "useful for finding out about library resources and services" and whether they would "ask a reference or research related question via Facebook" (Sachs, Eckel, and Langan 2011, 37). The results are inconclusive: the authors conclude that, although the libraries in the study have tried to use Facebook to answer reference questions, the primary function for a library Facebook page is for promotional and marketing purposes (48). Students are not necessarily thrilled with the idea of friending faculty and librarians, and if they do so, they simply want to be the recipient of information rather than seek information from the library (38–39). A recent article in the journal *Computers in Human Behavior* confirms that the three most popular activities on Facebook are "'viewing photos,' 'commenting on content' and 'checking to see what someone is up to'" (Junco 2012). The only mention of any academic activity comes in the last paragraph of the article, where the author observes that "a faculty member might create a Facebook group for a course and ask students to socialize about course content and share course-related information from news sources." Faculty, thus, can make Invisible Web content easier to access within such a Facebook group. Students can use databases for articles, magazines, and journals offered through the college or university simply by linking from Facebook to the sources via the local proxy system. Another article, "How Academic Libraries Reach Users on Facebook," studied the Facebook presence on the web of libraries which are members of the Association of Research Libraries. One of the observations is that on many Facebook pages, students have access to "third-party Facebook applications, such as WorldCat search, JSTOR and CiteMe" (Wan 2011, 316). This summarizes the limited use of Facebook for research purposes for the time being. There is no telling at this point in time whether Facebook will play a greater role in helping students link to Invisible Web content, either from institutional databases offered through the institution to those available freely on the web but not yet on students' radar.

The same can be said about the use of Twitter in academia. Thus far, Twitter is primarily used to converse within a class as described in chapter 2. It could conceivably be used in the same way as Facebook, with faculty members pointing students to Invisible Web content through tweets. There is no literature at the present documenting such use of Twitter.

CONCLUSION

We believe that educators must work with students in the environment we all live in today, meeting them "where they are at." This principle means not only not ruling out Google as a search tool but starting early, and starting by zeroing in on the basics of web searching. Instill good search skills that can be translated into every arena of life. Incrementally add more and more advanced skills and advocate the use of databases, introducing them by level of expertise, from kindergarten through college. In order to accomplish this tall agenda, all teachers, faculty, and librarians must be on board and collaborate. Social media may change the equation but, for the time being, such activity seems to be restricted to contacting friends or joining part of a small faculty-created group. Research is intricate and, unfortunately, time-consuming. But it can be fun, and an attitude of serendipity can be infused all along. Teaching about the Invisible Web should be part of every information literacy program. What makes a student a better researcher? In the words of Head and Eisenberg: "We argue evaluation, interpretation and synthesis are the key competencies of the 21st century. These information-literacy skills allow us to find what we need, filter out what we do not and chart a course in an ever-expanding frontier of information. Information literacy is the essential skill set that cuts across all disciplines and professions" (2011).

REFERENCES

Bergman, Michael K. 2001. "The Deep Web: Surfacing Hidden Value." Bright-Planet white paper, September 24. http://brightplanet.com/wp-content/uploads/2012/03/12550176481-deepwebwhitepaper1.pdf.

Boswell, Wendy. 2007. *The About.com Guide to Online Research: Navigate the Web—from RSS and the Invisible Web to Multimedia and the Blogosphere*. About.com Guides. Avon, MA: Adams Media.

De Rosa, Cathy, Joanne Cantrell, Matthew Carlson, Peggy Gallagher, Janet Hawk, and Charlotte Sturtz. 2010. *Perceptions of Libraries, 2010: Context and Community—a Report to the OCLC Membership*. Dublin, OH: OCLC.

Devine, Jane, and Francine Egger-Sider. 2009. *Going Beyond Google: The Invisible Web in Learning and Teaching*. New York: Neal-Schuman.

Du, Jia Tina, and Nina Evans. 2011. "Academic Users' Information Searching on Research Topics: Characteristics of Research Tasks and Search Strategies." *Journal of Academic Librarianship* 37, no. 4: 299–306. http://dx.doi.org/10.1016/j.acalib.2011.04.003.

Dubicki, Eleonora. 2010. "Research Behavior Patterns of Business Students." *Reference Services Review* 38, no. 3: 360–384. http://dx.doi.org/10.1108/00907321011070874.

Hampton-Reeves, Stuart, Claire Mashiter, Jonathan Westaway, Peter Lumsden, Helen Day, Helen Hewertson, et al. 2009. *Students' Use of Research Content in Teaching and Learning: A Report for the Joint Information Systems Council (JISC)*. Lancashire, UK: Centre for Research-Informed Teaching, University of Central Lancashire. www.jisc.ac.uk/media/documents/aboutus/workinggroups/studentsuseresearchcontent.pdf.

Hanson, Cody, Heather Hessel, Deborah Boudewyns, Janet Fransen, Lara Friedman-Shedlov, Stephen Hearn, et al. 2010. *Discoverability, Phase 2: Final Report*. Minneapolis, MN: University of Minnesota Libraries. http://conservancy.umn.edu/bitstream/99734/3/DiscoverabilityPhase2Report Full.pdf.

Harris, Robert. 2010. "Evaluating Internet Research Sources." *VirtualSalt*. www.virtualsalt.com/evalu8it.htm.

Head, Alison J., and Michael B. Eisenberg. 2009. *Finding Context: What Today's College Students Say about Conducting Research in the Digital Age*. Seattle, WA: Project Information Literacy, February 4. http://projectinfolit.org/pdfs/PIL_ProgressReport_2_2009.pdf.

———. 2010. *Truth Be Told: How College Students Evaluate and Use Information in the Digital Age*. Seattle, WA: Project Information Literacy, November 1. http://projectinfolit.org/pdfs/PIL_Fall2010_Survey_FullReport1.pdf.

———. 2011. "College Students Eager to Learn but Need Help Negotiating Information Overload." *Seattle Times*, June 3. http://seattletimes.nwsource.com/html/opinion/2015227485_guest05head.html.

Heiberger, Greg, and Reynol Junco. 2011. "Meet Your Students Where They Are: Social Media." *NEA Higher Education Advocate* 28, no. 5: 6–9. www.nea.org/assets/img/PubAdvocate/Advocate_sept11.pdf.

Judd, Terry, and Gregor Kennedy. 2011. "Expediency-Based Practice? Medical Students' Reliance on Google and Wikipedia for Biomedical Inquiries." *British Journal of Educational Technology* 42, no. 2: 351–360. http://dx.doi.org/10.1111/j.1467-8535.2009.01019.x.

Junco, Reynol. 2012. "Too Much Face and Not Enough Books: The Relationship between Multiple Indices of Facebook Use and Academic Performance." *Computers in Human Behavior* 28, no. 1: 187–198. http://dx.doi.org/10.1016/j.chb.2011.08.026.

Kolowich, Steve. 2009. "Behind New Online College and University Rankings." *Chronicle of Higher Education*, January 8. http://chronicle.com/blogs/wiredcampus/behind-new-online-collegeuniversity-rankings/4461.

Kuhlthau, Carol Collier. 2004. *Seeking Meaning: A Process Approach to Library and Information Services*. 2nd ed. Westport, CT: Libraries Unlimited.

Matthew, Victoria, and Ann Schroeder. 2006. "The Embedded Librarian Program." *EDUCAUSE Quarterly* 29, no. 4. www.educause.edu/ero/article/embedded-librarian-program.

Notess, Greg R. 2006. *Teaching Web Search Skills: Techniques and Strategies of Top Trainers*. Medford, NJ: Information Today.

Nutefall, Jennifer E., and Phyllis Mentzell Ryder. 2010. "The Serendipitous Research Process." *Journal of Academic Librarianship* 36, no. 3: 228–234. http://dx.doi.org/10.1016/j.acalib.2010.03.005.

Sachs, Dianna E., Edward J. Eckel, and Kathleen A. Langan. 2011. "Striking a Balance: Effective Use of Facebook in an Academic Library." *Internet Reference Services Quarterly* 16, no. 1–2: 35–54. http://dx.doi.org/10.1080/10875301.2011 .572457.

Sherman, Chris, and Gary Price. 2001. *The Invisible Web: Uncovering Information Sources Search Engines Can't See*. Medford, NJ: CyberAge Books.

Singhal, Amit, and Matt Cutts. 2011. "Finding More High-Quality Sites in Search." *The Official Google Blog*, February 24. googleblog.blogspot.com/2011/02/ finding-more-high-quality-sites-in.html.

Smith, Shannon D., and Judith Borreson Caruso. 2010. *The ECAR Study of Under- graduate Students and Information Technology, 2010*. Boulder, CO: EDUCAUSE. http://net.educause.edu/ir/library/pdf/ERS1006/RS/ERS1006W.pdf.

Sullivan, Danny. 2011. "Google Forecloses on Content Farms with 'Panda' Algorithm Update." *Search Engine Land* (blog), February 24. http:// searchengineland.com/google-forecloses-on-content-farms-with-farmer -algorithm-update-66071.

Timpson, Helen, and Gemma Sansom. 2011. "A Student Perspective on e-Resource Discovery: Has the Google Factor Changed Publisher Platform Searching Forever?" *Serials Librarian* 61, no. 2: 253–266. http://dx.doi.org/10.1080/ 0361526X.2011.592115.

Wan, Gang (Gary). 2011. "How Academic Libraries Reach Users on Facebook." *College & Undergraduate Libraries* 18, no. 4: 307–318. http://dx.doi.org/10.1080/ 10691316.2011.624944.

Wikipedia. 2011. S.v. "Principle of Least Effort." Last modified November 10. http://en.wikipedia.org/wiki/Principle_of_least_effort.

TEACHING RESOURCES

KNOWLEDGE OF THE INVISIBLE WEB PROVIDES students with a better understanding of the rich web information world and, therefore, warrants attention in information literacy programs. An important point to remember about teaching information literacy is that, in addition to the larger opportunities of a class session on research or a library workshop, there are many smaller teachable moments; this applies to teaching about the Invisible Web as well. Small teaching moments help support the larger efforts by reinforcing the ideas about the information world and research skills that students need. Thus mentioning the Invisible Web when introducing someone to a subscription database at a reference desk counts. Comparing databases with a Google search, as we did in chapter 4, also contributes. Anything that can help broaden students' perspective of the web information world helps create better-informed researchers. The Invisible Web can be taught, not as a replacement for Google, but as a set of resources that complement those covered by Google. The Invisible Web need not be presented as some "other" entity but rather, along with Google, as a part of the information world as a whole.

It never hurts to have a strategy and some tools at hand to help capitalize on teaching opportunities as they arise. This chapter offers a sampling of resources that can help introduce students to the Invisible Web. Some tools were already showcased in chapter 4 in the context of curricular levels, and the resources suggested here are intended to supplement that discussion. Many of these tools reflect ideas offered by survey participants as their way of introducing the Invisible Web to their students. Some respondents began with a graphic to convey an image of the Invisible Web. A popular strategy involved inserting the idea of the Invisible Web when introducing students to subscription databases. Explaining that databases reach into material that general-purpose search engines cannot obtain can be an effective hook to get students' attention. Some survey takers introduced the Invisible Web when talking about Google and search engines in general. Grasping all these teaching moments is positive pedagogy; not doing so is a disservice to students.

INFORMATION CONTEXT OVERVIEW

As we have learned in the previous chapters, students can become discouraged and confused when seeking information on the web. They are overwhelmed by all the resources they find because all the information looks alike to them. Hence they need context as well as the evaluation skills discussed in the previous chapter. They need to understand why there are different forms of information and what each contributes to the whole picture. A video created as a tutorial by the University Libraries at Pennsylvania State University in 2004, "The Information Cycle," continues to serve as a good introduction (see the original at www.libraries.psu.edu/content/dam/psul/up/lls/audiovideo/infocycle_2008.swf or the 2011 redesign for YouTube available at http://youtu.be/klrKEMIa1X4). This video follows the various types of information created about a news event—in this case the Columbine school shootings in 1999—as time progresses, from the initial reporting on television, radio, and the Internet, to next-day newspaper reporting, to journal articles appearing later with analysis of the event, and finally to books that offer in-depth analysis and overview. Students need to see these differences, which will help them to make choices among all the different forms of resources available to them on the web, including e-books and articles. The only element missing from "The Information Cycle" is an exploration of social media. Twitter and Pinterest did not yet exist and Facebook was only getting started when the video was created, but they have played important roles in various recent news stories such as the Arab Spring. Students can be guided to consider this type of social media reporting as a primary source of firsthand information, with the understanding that other kinds of sources are needed for balance. The Penn State video does not identify the Invisible Web specifically, but it provides a teaching moment to mention it in conjunction with the articles, books, and websites referred to. For example, teachers might work with their students to create their own information cycle as an assignment or class project built around a current news event. Knowing more about information formats and source types will enable students to proceed faster with their report assignments, and as the record in chapter 2 shows, the ability to work quickly is valuable to them.

The following resources also discuss information formats and types. They may not mention the Invisible Web, but they offer the opportunity to do so in a class follow-up.

"EXPLORE SOURCES: TYPES OF INFORMATION" (2009)

www.clark.edu/Library/iris/types/sources/sources.shtml

This tutorial reviews types of information sources including broadcast media, newspapers, articles, and books, and their characteristics (fig. 5.1). A companion tutorial on "The Deep Web" is available at www.clark.edu/Library/iris/types/deep_web/deep_web.shtml. *Sponsored by Clark College Libraries*

"TYPES OF INFORMATION SOURCES" (2010)

http://youtu.be/C5bNS82sE5c

This video gives an in-depth review of books, reference titles, magazines, journals, and the web as information source types. It refers to "The Information Cycle." Length: 7 minutes, 31 seconds. *Western Nevada College Library*

FIGURE 5.1 Explore Sources: Types of Information

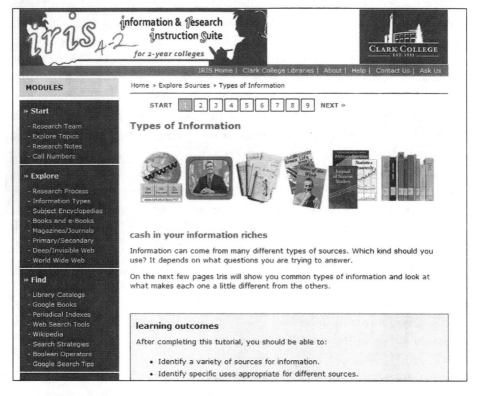

Source: Clark College, www.clark.edu/Library/iris/types/sources/sources.shtml. Used by permission.

INTRODUCING THE INVISIBLE WEB WITH GRAPHICS

Helping students visualize the web world of information and the part that the Invisible Web plays is important. Several respondents to question 9 of our survey, asking how they introduce the Invisible Web when teaching (chapter 3), said that they do so with a graphic. The most popular image was that of an iceberg, as mentioned in chapter 4. This image has long been a favorite way of showing the idea that the web is really made up of easily found resources (the surface web, or the part of the iceberg above water) and less easily found materials (below the water line) that are hidden from general-purpose search engines. The iceberg image can easily be used in any classroom; after all, anyone should be able to draw a triangle with one peak showing above the water line and the larger section appearing below. The web abounds with examples of iceberg graphics used by various websites or for presentations about the Invisible Web. A quick Google Image search (yes, Google!) for "iceberg and Invisible Web" (no quotation marks) will offer many choices. There is always the risk that students may remember only the iceberg and not what it was intended to represent, so using the image does require explanation.

Here is an example of an iceberg image:

GRAPHIC—ICEBERG (2011)

www.web.archive.org/web/*/http://www.nvcc.edu/annandale/library/research/media/ppt/library-research.ppt

This iceberg image is part of a PowerPoint presentation on doing research created by Kevin Simons (fig. 5.2). It does a good job of presenting the ideas that should help define the surface and Invisible Web. The concepts that appear on the graphic, such as not organized versus organized, free versus $$$$ (fee-based) resources, Google versus more sophisticated search tools, provide ample opportunities for discussion. *By Kevin E. Simons, Northern Virginia Community College*

FIGURE 5.2 Graphic—iceberg

Kevin E. Simons, reprinted by permission.

Split-Level Searching: Finding Niche Tools

Niche tools represent an interesting aspect of searching. They can be found using general-purpose search engines. A searcher, for instance, might search a subject area and add "databases" to the search terms (e.g., community colleges and databases) to locate specialized databases. This process is called *split-level searching.* Once this preliminary search has identified more specialized tools, the searcher can begin a secondary search step using those tools to continue the research.

An effective class assignment might be to ask students to do a search using Google and then redo the search adding "databases" to the keyword terms and compare the results.

OTHER GRAPHICS/OTHER IMAGES

Another popular image used to show the Invisible Web is that of the ocean and a fishing vessel whose nets may only reach shallow water, representing the surface web. This image was made famous (at least in the world of information technology) in Michael Bergman's white paper, "The Deep Web: Surfacing Hidden Value" (2001), which helped define the Invisible Web for many people. The ship's nets are shown to fish the surface indiscriminately, leaving behind the many deeper catches which are the Invisible Web's riches. A companion image shows ships with deeper nets more successfully reaching those deep resources.

Here is another image based on this theme:

"HOW DEEP IS YOUR WEB" (2011)

http://brandpowder.wordpress.com/2011/10/03/how-deep-is-your-web
Appearing in a blog posting dated October 3, 2011, this graphic (fig. 5.3) features explanatory labels worth reading. While the ocean imagery continues in the Bergman tradition, it is also an updated view of the information world, with a nod to the cloud and an allusion to the dark web that is part of the Invisible Web (Muttoni 2011). *From* Brandpowder, *a blog site featuring graphics*

FIGURE 5.3 "How Deep Is Your Web"

Source: Brandpowder: Experiments in Visual Communication,
http://brandpowder.wordpress.com.

DIAGRAMS

Finally, there are diagrams of the whole web that also suggest the scope and contents of the Invisible Web. Like the iceberg and fishing images, these diagrams convey the size of the Invisible Web in proportion to the surface web but not necessarily the value of its resources. Giving a sense of the value of these information resources can be an important teaching moment for the classroom. Diagrams come in many forms, of which a few have been selected for inclusion here.

"THE FOUR CONTENT LAYERS OF THE WORLD WIDE WEB" (2005)

http://netforbeginners.about.com/library/diagrams/n4layers.htm
Paul Gil has created a diagram of the World Wide Web content in layers, with the Invisible Web representing the most prominent part of the image. The diagram clearly shows niche tools as reaching down from the surface web to include Invisible Web materials. This image, which has become a sort of classic visualization of the web, appeared in our first book (Devine and Egger-Sider 2009). *By Paul Gil, as part of the About.com "Internet for Beginners" guide*

FIGURE 5.4 **Graphic—The Four Content Layers of the World Wide Web**

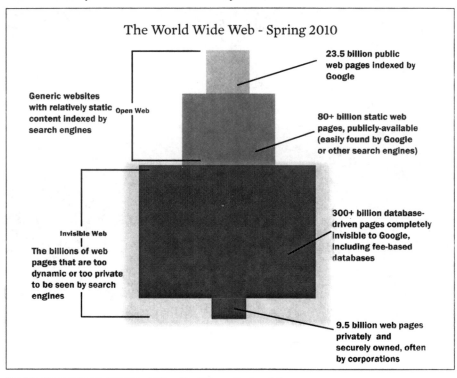

The World Wide Web - Spring 2010

23.5 billion public web pages indexed by Google

Generic websites with relatively static content indexed by search engines — Open Web

80+ billion static web pages, publicly-available (easily found by Google or other search engines)

300+ billion database-driven pages completely invisible to Google, including fee-based databases

Invisible Web

The billions of web pages that are too dynamic or too private to be seen by search engines

9.5 billion web pages privately and securely owned, often by corporations

Reprinted by permission, Harold and Wilma Good Library, Goshen College.

"BEYOND GOOGLING: THE INVISIBLE WEB" (2010)

http://goshen.libguides.com/beyond_googling

This image (fig. 5.4) represents another interpretation, based on Paul Gil's data for About.com. The image is part of a guide about the Invisible Web. *By N. Tann, for the Harold and Wilma Good Library, Goshen College*

"INVISIBLE WEB" (2011)

http://libguides.uky.edu/content.php?pid=53054&sid=1992304&search_terms=invisible+web

This image, similar to a Venn diagram, shows circles of information for the Invisible Web and what it calls the "open web." *By Chris Worland, for University of Kentucky Libraries*

"USING THE METAPHOR OF THE 'DEEP' OR 'INVISIBLE' WEB" (2009)
www.slideshare.net/kimduckett/deep-web-diagram
This is actually a slide show showing a progression of five slides starting with the surface web and adding the layers down to the Invisible Web. It shows Invisible Web information residing in information silos, including free and fee-based resources. *By Kim Duckett of North Carolina State University and Scott Warren of Syracuse University*

Information Silos

The term *information silos* can be used to explain why some information is inaccessible to general-purpose search engines. Silos are storage structures, and to gain access to their content, you must use each one's individual door. In the same vein, databases are best accessed using their own search functions. Many students have no idea how information is stored and made accessible on the web. Planting the idea in students' heads that they may need to be prepared to search individual databases for certain topics, using those databases' own search protocols, is a big step toward information literacy.

USING VIDEOS TO INTRODUCE THE INVISIBLE WEB

Videos provide another means to introduce the Invisible Web and at the same time connect with students who enjoy YouTube. We've already discussed "The Information Cycle." Here are some other resources that educate as well as entertain.

"DEEP WEB" (2009)
http://youtu.be/L8X5uMUPQYU
This video provides a quick view of searching the Invisible Web, as contrasted with Google and the surface web, for scientific information. The video promotes Invisible Web search tools that OSTI has helped develop, such as Science.gov (www.science.gov), Science Accelerator (www.science accelerator.gov), and WorldWideScience.org (www.worldwidescience.org). These search tools utilize the *federated* search concept, whereby one search

interface searches several databases, usually all selected with a common subject matter. The federal government is a large producer of Invisible Web content, and these tools help researchers find government publications. Length: 2 minutes, 13 seconds. *Produced by the Office of Scientific and Technical Information (OSTI), which is part of the U.S. Department of Energy*

Federated Searching

Federated searching was discussed in the previous chapter and will be reviewed again in chapter 6 with examples of federated search tools. Federated searches are analogous to metasearch engines, which search across several search engines at once, but they apply to databases rather than to search engines. Students who already use metasearch tools like Dogpile may find that federating searching appeals to them and is less exotic than it might at first seem.

"SEARCHING THE DEEP WEB" (2009)
http://youtu.be/LPUgxQDd88w

This video is also produced by OSTI to give a more complete description of the differences between a surface search engine such as Google and one of OSTI's sponsored search tools, Science.gov (www.science.gov). It mentions real-time searching and the ability to search across several databases at one time (federated searching). Length: 6 minutes, 10 seconds. *Produced by OSTI*

"SEARCHING WITH SUCCESS!" (2004)
http://library.acadiau.ca/tutorials/websearching

This animated tutorial explains basic search skills and follows the experiences of three students with research projects. A section on the Deep Web (Invisible Web) utilizes the ocean metaphor. The tutorial asks questions along the way and explains all the answers. The animation may appeal to younger users. Length: Approximately 10 minutes. *Vaughn Memorial Library, Acadia University*

"EXPLORING THE DEEP WEB" (2011)
http://youtu.be/AQ9iblkb57I

This video does a good job of explaining the Invisible Web. It includes a section on the darknet or dark web. Length: 14 minutes, 42 seconds. *By Dan Downs*

"WHAT IS THE DEEP WEB?" (2011)

http://youtu.be/YM6kvccqV4c

In explaining the content of the Invisible Web, this video uses the imagery of both the iceberg and the ocean. The explanation is offered in an entertaining way. Length: 4 minutes, 46 seconds. *By Chris Krause*

COMPARE AND CONTRAST

Many survey respondents said they introduce the Invisible Web with compare-and-contrast activities, often during a session on search engines or on databases. Getting students to consider using databases as a second resource after trying Google and, eventually, as a first resource is an important effort. Lessons and assignments that ask students to compare the results from a database with those from a search engine are probably the most common way to introduce students to this broader view. The comparisons offered in chapter 4 demonstrate what this type of activity will show. A class session may end with compiling a list or chart of the characteristics of a database as opposed to a search engine to help illustrate their differences. We included a comparison chart in our first book (Devine and Egger-Sider 2009), and others exist on the web for reference.

Here are a few examples:

"HOW DATABASES AND SEARCH ENGINES DIFFER" (2011)

www.library.illinois.edu/ugl/howdoi/compare1.html

This table is a basic comparison of databases and search engines. *University Library, University of Illinois at Urbana-Champaign*

"LIBRARY DATABASES VS. SEARCH ENGINES" (2011)

http://libguides.reynolds.edu/content.php?pid=81682&sid=611876

This table, part of a library research guide, contrasts the types of information found by databases and search engines and discusses usability and source citation. *J. Sargeant Reynolds Community College Library*

Real-Time Searching

Real-time searching occurs when a search tool actually goes out on the web to find resources that exist at the time of the query. Most general-purpose search engines do not offer real-time searching, except perhaps for news and Twitter postings. Search engines can produce quick answers by having pre-searched (i.e., indexed) results ready for the user. Real-time searching would require a much longer response time, especially as the web is growing each day.

Most real-time search tools search only a limited number of resources, which they name clearly, in order to produce a reasonably fast result. Topsy (www.topsy .com) is an example of a real-time search tool.

"SEARCH ENGINE VS. RESEARCH DATABASE FOR COLLEGE RESEARCH" (2009)

http://youtu.be/VUp1P-ubOlc

This short video does a good job of presenting the differences between databases and search engines as research tools. Length: 1 minute, 58 seconds. *Modesto Junior College*

If you do assign a comparison activity, remember that general-purpose search engines can do quite a good job of presenting results for purely scholarly topics, which do not attract much interest for commercial enterprises.

INTRODUCING THE INVISIBLE WEB WITH TUTORIALS AND GUIDES

Some respondents to the Invisible Web survey mentioned using guides and providing links to Invisible Web materials. Many such resources are available on the web; here are some that we would recommend.

"THE DEEP WEB" (2013)

www.web.archive.org/web/20130062015752/http://internettutorials.net/deepweb.asp

This tutorial has been one of the best about the Invisible Web. Taken off the open web in June 2013, it continues to be helpful and available in the Internet Archive. *By Laura B. Cohen, Internet Tutorials*

"WHAT IS THE INVISIBLE WEB? HOW CAN YOU SEARCH IT? WHY WOULD YOU WANT TO?" (2003–2005)

http://21cif.com/tutorials/micro/mm/invisible

This is a seven-screen tutorial. The third screen provides a link to a video called "Using Search Engines to Find Invisible Web Resources." Screen four offers another video, "Using the Advanced Features of a Search Engine to Find Invisible Web Content." The site uses illustrations that should appeal to younger audiences. The 21st Century Information Fluency Project is dedicated to furthering online information literacy and offers many other tutorials and resources for teaching information literacy. The final tutorial page offers links to these other resources and a search function for the site. A search for "Invisible Web" will bring up other resources offered by 21st Century Information Fluency. *By Dennis O'Connor, for the 21st Century Information Fluency Project*

"INVISIBLE OR DEEP WEB: WHAT IT IS, HOW TO FIND IT, AND ITS INHERENT AMBIGUITY" (2010)

http://library.berkeley.edu/TeachingLib/Guides/Internet/InvisibleWeb.html

A classic among Invisible Web guides. Originally developed in 2000 by Joe Barker, this tutorial continues to be updated and is an excellent introductory resource. *University of California, Berkeley Library*

"SEARCHING THE DEEP WEB" (2011)

http://library.stevens.edu/content.php?pid=159078&search_terms=invisible+web

This guide provides a list of links to Invisible Web resources arranged by source type and subject. *S. C. Williams Library, Stevens Institute of Technology*

"THE SECRET WEB" (2011)

http://lanecc.libguides.com/secretweb

Using the handle "secret web," this guide reviews materials that fall into the Invisible Web. *Lane Community College Library*

ADDITIONAL RESOURCES RELATED TO THE INVISIBLE WEB

Here are some additional resources that relate to issues mentioned in this book and that might supplement class discussions about the Invisible Web.

"THE FILTER BUBBLE: HOW THE HIDDEN WEB IS SHAPING LIVES" (2011)
http://youtu.be/6_sim_Wc3mY
This is a video of a talk given by Eli Pariser, author of a book with the same title. He discusses the personalization features used by search engines and what that process means to researchers. See chapter 2 for a discussion of filtering and how it relates to the Invisible Web. Length: 24 minutes, 54 seconds. *Sponsored by the Royal Society for the Encouragement of Arts, Manufacture and Commerce (RSA Organization)*

"WEB 3.0" (2011)
http://vimeo.com/11529540
This video explores the potential of the Semantic Web and features Tim Berners-Lee, creator of the World Wide Web, Alon Halevy, a Google research scientist, and others taking a critical view of what the Semantic Web may be able to accomplish. There will be more discussion of the Semantic Web in chapter 7. Length: 14 minutes, 25 seconds. *Source: Kate Ray*

"TIMELINE OF EVENTS RELATED TO THE DEEP WEB" (2008)
http://papergirls.wordpress.com/2008/10/07/timeline-deep-web
While this timeline has not been kept up-to-date, it still offers a good look at how the Invisible Web has long been part of the World Wide Web. *By Maureen Flynn-Burhoe*

"SOCIAL BOOKMARKING" (2012)
http://libguides.geneseo.edu/content.php?pid=114468&sid=989448
Most students already participate in some form of social media such as Facebook, but fewer use social bookmarking sites. This guide offers some information and links to videos about how to get started in social bookmarking. *Milne Library, State University of New York at Geneseo*

Chapter 6 will offer a sampler of tools that can help the researcher find Invisible Web resources.

REFERENCES

Bergman, Michael K. 2001. "The Deep Web: Surfacing Hidden Value." Bright-Planet white paper, September 24. http://brightplanet.com/wp-content/uploads/2012/03/12550176481-deepwebwhitepaper1.pdf.

Muttoni, Carlo. 2011. "How Deep Is Your Web." *Brandpowder: Experiments in Visual Communication* (blog). October 3. http://brandpowder.wordpress.com/2011/10/03/how-deep-is-your-web.

Devine, Jane, and Francine Egger-Sider. 2009. *Going Beyond Google: The Invisible Web in Learning and Teaching.* New York: Neal-Schuman.

Pariser, Eli. 2011. *The Filter Bubble: What the Internet Is Hiding from You.* New York: Penguin.

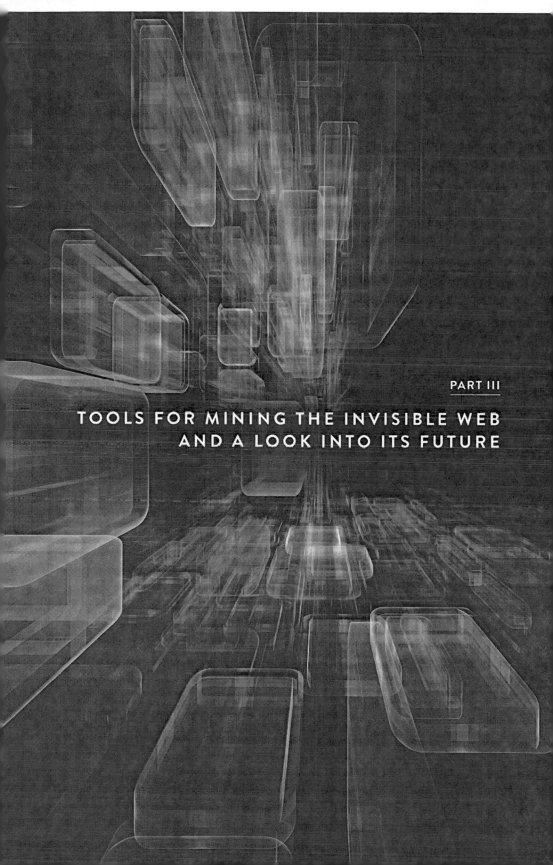

PART III

TOOLS FOR MINING THE INVISIBLE WEB
AND A LOOK INTO ITS FUTURE

LOOKING INSIDE THE
INVISIBLE WEB: A SAMPLER

HAPTER 1 EXPLORED THE CHARACTERISTICS of the Invisible Web, and this chapter will build on those characteristics to explore research tools that find information in the Invisible Web. Chapter 1 placed Invisible Web resources as complementary to those found by general-purpose search engines such as Google, Yahoo, and Bing. Invisible Web resources complete the picture of the web information world. It seems unlikely that people will give up their reliance on general-purpose search engines or their practice of beginning a search using Google or one of its competitors. Today, these are part of everyone's basic research tool kit.

However, people should be encouraged to take the next step when needed and use other research tools such as databases and more specialized search engines—that is, Invisible Web resources. These, too, can be part of the basic research tool kit. It is clear that students can benefit from using the subscription databases offered to them by their schools and libraries. Those subscription databases have been chosen to meet student research needs and can ultimately save students time and effort. For some course work, especially in fields such as nursing that require regular reviews by accrediting agencies, subject databases are a requirement. Many students, as they move through their education and into their professional lives, will need ever more specialized, sophisticated tools to fill their research demands. At this stage, the Invisible Web takes the form of advanced search resources. This chapter will help define the basic and advanced search possibilities of the Invisible Web.

One of the characteristics of the Invisible Web, as discussed in chapter 1, is that it is not widely known. It is, therefore, easy for the Invisible Web to be dismissed as a set of remote information resources that only specialists will need to know about or use. While this view may be accurate for some of the Invisible Web, we want to create a different impression. It may be effective at this point to conjure up again the image of the iceberg that is so often used to visualize the web information world and the Invisible Web's place in it (see chapter 5). The surface web and the Invisible Web meet at the water line and, even at that point, there are many Invisible Web resources that are useful to everyone, including students. This upper layer of the Invisible Web might be called the "basic research tool kit" zone. Deeper into the water there is another zone of more specialized resources that are more meaningful for people in specific fields of study or occupations. Finally, the Invisible Web comprises a third zone of even more specialized tools that will probably be useful only to particular research communities, archivists, and the like. We will explore the resources in all of these zones. Table 6.1 summarizes the characteristics of the three zones or layers of the Invisible Web and lists examples of their content.

What makes each of the suggested research tools "Invisible Web tools" is their ability to uncover resources that general-purpose search engines cannot. As we saw in chapter 1, resources that make up the Invisible Web include dynamic content, sources found through proprietary databases, new and unusual formats, material found deep in rich websites, very current resources, unlinked materials, and fee-based content. The search tools reviewed below are each located within their appropriate layer of broad or specialized usefulness and tagged with their Invisible Web properties (see table 6.2). This review is intended to provide only selective examples of several kinds of research tools rather than a comprehensive list. The fine resources recommended in our first book (Devine and Egger-Sider 2009, 93–107) are not duplicated here.

TABLE 6.1
Layers of the Invisible Web

First layer: basic research tool kit	Basic research tools can help anyone with general research and, in the case of students, with assignments. A basic research tool kit should include the following: • General reference tools, including subscription and free dynamic-content databases • Data and statistics resources • Access to magazines and journals • News sources • Everyday life resources (popular interest)
Second layer: specialized research	These are tools for specialized research (think vertical): • Subscription and free dynamic-content databases • Subject-themed search engines • Access to academic journals • Specialized graphics and media • Social bookmarking sites
Third layer: advanced research	This layer includes very specialized materials (think niche): • Databases • Repository collections • Hard-to-find formats • Niche tools • Special research communities

TABLE 6.2
Tags applicable to Invisible Web resources

Tools described in this chapter will be tagged with the properties that define them as part of the Invisible Web.

Introduced in chapter 1	• Currency—news • Dynamic content • Fee-based • Formats, new or unusual • Niche • Unique materials not found or linked to elsewhere • Vertical
Introduced in chapter 5	• Federated searching • Real-time searching

BASIC RESEARCH TOOLS

The exploration of basic tools can begin with databases, which are at the heart of the Invisible Web. Proprietary databases and those that provide answers dynamically are Invisible Web resources. Databases offer vetted resources that must conform to an editorial standard and therefore differ from general-purpose search engines. Users do have to work through the database's own search functions, which may not be as simply laid out as the Google search box. General-purpose search engines do not include the content of these databases in their results list, with the possible exception of Google Scholar, which has agreements with some proprietary databases that permit it to include references to the database content but not the full text.

Proprietary databases are fee-based or subscription products but many are offered by libraries at no additional charge to their communities. In *Going Beyond Google*, we profiled LexisNexis Academic as an example of such a subscription database, and it remains a valuable choice. Others include general-purpose EBSCOhost databases such as Academic Search Complete, and products from providers like ProQuest and Gale. In most cases, the databases provide access to magazine and journal articles useful for students and for anyone with everyday life research needs.

The content of open-access databases built to provide dynamic answers in real time are not included in general-purpose search engine indexing and are part of the Invisible Web.

Also included in this review of resources are search engines, a repository collection, statistics and data resources, and more. The resources are organized first by usefulness for students and then for everyday purposes.

STUDENT RESEARCH

VOICE OF THE SHUTTLE (VOS): WEBSITE FOR HUMANITIES SEARCH

http://vos.ucsb.edu

Sponsored by the English Department of the University of California at Santa Barbara, Voice of the Shuttle (VoS) was started by Professor Alan Liu in 1994. It describes itself as a dynamic database of online resources on literature, the humanities, cultural studies, and much more. VoS includes both primary and secondary resources and offers links to course materials, author websites, literature in English and other languages, and e-books. The user can search by titles of works, author names, or broad subjects. The dynamic structure of VoS and the inclusion of difficult-to-find resources make it an example of an Invisible Web database. Its subject coverage makes it especially useful for students. *Tags: dynamic content, unique materials not linked elsewhere*

BIZNAR: DEEP WEB BUSINESS SEARCH
http://biznar.com

A product of Deep Web Technologies, this search engine scans all kinds of resources, including periodicals such as *Advertising Age*, government resources such as USA.gov and the Bureau of Labor Statistics, the news sources *Business Week* and the *Wall Street Journal*, social networks like *LinkedIn* and *Wordpress*, and many more resources listed under the advanced search option. BizNar represents an example of federated search, which is an approach to accessing materials related to a broad subject, in this case business, by targeting a range of specially selected databases and search engines. Searching is done at the time of the query on a real-time basis, and results offer links to full text and topic clusters to select from. BizNar is a good general resource that covers all aspects of the business world. *Tags: dynamic content, federated search, real-time search, vertical*

INTERNET ARCHIVE
www.archive.org

Home of the Wayback Machine, the Internet Archive is a large repository dedicated to preserving the digital world and offering access to its past through a publicly accessible library. Many researchers have had the experience of losing a web resource. Hoping to use it again, they have been dismayed to find that it is no longer accessible. In some cases, the Internet Archive may offer access to that lost resource, having preserved it in its collection. While not fully comprehensive, the collections do a great job of preserving much of the early web for posterity. These resources do not appear on Google search results lists; users must navigate the Internet Archive's own search function. Users can search by subject, by the URL of the site that has disappeared from the web, and by media type. The Internet Archive is a nonprofit organization. *Tags: unique materials not found or linked to elsewhere*

DATA.GOV: EMPOWERING PEOPLE, AN OFFICIAL WEBSITE OF THE UNITED STATES GOVERNMENT

www.data.gov

A very good source of data for student reports or business or general information purposes is the U.S. Federal Government, which collects all kinds of data. Government sources are often Invisible Web materials because they are buried deep in massive websites and because the government is the unique source for important research and information. Statistical data can be found across many government department websites, but it may be hard to track down with a search. For example, the U.S. Census Bureau website (www.census.gov) can dynamically generate statistical reports about many topics. Data.gov is another way to tap government statistical reporting. It searches across U.S. government databases for reports, articles, and data. A simple keyword search produces results with links and descriptions. It also offers tools to use the data. *Tags: federated searching, unique materials not found or linked to elsewhere*

EVERYDAY LIFE AIDS

PIPL: PEOPLE SEARCH

http://pipl.com

Pipl, sponsored by a search engine company with the same name, identifies itself as the most comprehensive people search on the web. It claims that its success is due to the fact that its taps Invisible Web resources, where a lot of people information is kept; however, it does not list the sources that it relies on. Search results do link to where the source of the information resides. Some sources offer detailed information for a fee. Pipl is a useful tool for anyone trying to locate a lost friend or colleague. *Tags: vertical*

MEDNAR: DEEP WEB MEDICAL SEARCH

http://mednar.com

Like BizNar, MedNar has been developed by Deep Web Technologies. It is a free, publicly available Invisible Web search engine that utilizes federated search for medical resources. A list of the specific sites searched by MedNar is available under the advanced search option; it includes many government sites and medical societies and some commercial databases. Search results show the particular collections searched and the number of results found in each collection. Or a search can be limited to one collection if the user so wishes. Results include an article link and source information. A topic breakdown for the search also appears to the left of the screen, which provides the number of articles available for each related topic. MedNar does real-time searching—actually searching at the time of the query—so that, as a result, its response time may be slower than that of a Google-type search engine which provides previously assembled search results. MedNar can also be labeled a vertical search engine, one that reviews a subject area deeply. It can help students or anyone seeking health-related information. *Tags: dynamic content, federated search, real-time search, vertical*

SCOUT.ME
www.scout.me

A product of TeleNav, this search tool deals with leisure-time activities and helps users find activities and entertainment in their area. Users can type in an idea or select from a list of possibilities, give a desired location, and receive information about options. Results include all the information needed to participate in the activity. This tool is an example of a niche search tool; it does one thing well, searches deeply, and provides information that is current and would be hard to locate using general-purpose search engines. *Tags: niche*

YUMMLY: EVERY RECIPE IN THE WORLD
www.yummly.com

Yummly offers the searcher the opportunity to look for recipes and select from various search result options that include ingredients, cooking time, directions, and the source for the recipe. Additional ways to search include by national cuisines, allergies, and holidays. Yummly searches not only for keywords but for context and intent, utilizing a semantic approach which is explained in more depth in a blog posting by Erica Ogg (2011). *Tags: vertical*

TOPSY: REAL-TIME SEARCH FOR
THE SOCIAL WEB (TWITTER, GOOGLE+, VIDEO)
http://topsy.com

Created by Topsy Labs, an indexing technology company, Topsy can be searched in general or more specifically by links, tweets, photos, videos, experts, and what it calls "trending." The search engine taps Twitter, Goo-gle+, and video sources like YouTube, and offers resources in several lan-guages. The first screen features trending items: news tweets from the last few minutes as well as postings from news sites and blogs. A user can do a subject search and receive results which can be sorted by time periods that range from the last hour, day, week, thirty days, or more. An "expert" search allows the user to search a subject and get results for people who have been posting on that topic along with analytics on how often the search terms appear in an individual's postings. There are links to the poster and any sto-ries that mention the search term. *Tags: real-time search*

POPURLS:
GENUINE AGGREGATOR

http://popurls.com

Popurls offers a collection of headlines, news, and web buzz from a cross section of sources that include Reddit, YouTube, and the *New York Times*. The user can check favorites and scan many other resources all on one page. After displaying the headlines from the most popular sites, Popurls provides a breakdown of additional sources and stories by categories such as News and Magazines, Politics, Business and Finance, Women, Sports, and the like. Popurls is a good general purpose aggregator site. *Tags: currency—news*.

SOCIAL MENTION:
REAL-TIME SOCIAL MEDIA SEARCH AND ANALYSIS

www.socialmention.com

A social media aggregator, Social Mention reviews user-generated content from over 80 sources. Users have the option to select only those kinds of sites they want to target or search all of them at once. The options include blogs, microblogs, bookmarking sites, and more. Search results show links to postings, where and when they were made, and all kinds of analytics of the search results. *Tags: real-time search*

SECOND LAYER TOOLS

Beyond popular and basic reference tools, there are many other tools that can assist those with more specialized needs. These resources are more academic in nature, and the Invisible Web abounds with them, from proprietary databases to fee-based resources that cover in depth almost any subject area, especially in the sciences. Subscription databases that cover one subject rather than serving as general-purpose research tools fall into this layer of the Invisible Web. Examples include services such as Elsevier's ScienceDirect; CINAHL, a medical database for Nursing and Allied Health students; and ERIC—Education Resources Information Center, which is available both through subscription and as an open-access database. This second layer of Invisible Web resources also includes subject-based search engines, academic periodical collections, and image collections. Here is a selection.

WORLDWIDESCIENCE.ORG: THE GLOBAL SCIENCE GATEWAY
http://worldwidescience.org

This database is the product of an alliance among international scientific institutions and is operated by the United States Department of Energy. It can be searched in many languages and offers translations. It also offers a list of all the institutional collections included and is a focused federated tool that searches across all of these holdings. Searches may also be limited to specific collections. A regular search produces references with author, title, and collection where the document resides. Full text is offered for many but not all documents. The materials offered include conference papers, articles, and other documents not readily found on the surface web. *Tags: federated search, real-time search, unique resources not found or linked to elsewhere*

NEW YORK PUBLIC LIBRARY DIGITAL GALLERY
http://digitalgallery.nypl.org

This image collection offers digitized copies of the many rare and unusual holdings of the New York Public Library, including historical documents, images, photographs, art pieces, maps, and more. The collection covers all subject areas with over 700,000 images that can be searched by keyword or browsed by subject. Items can be printed out or the user can order high-quality reproductions. The library indicates clearly that some images may require copyright approval for use, but it supplies all the information needed to secure that approval. This site can help with history assignments or may be useful to anyone seeking historical images. *Tags: unique materials not found or linked to elsewhere*

DEEPDYVE

www.deepdyve.com

DeepDyve, a fee-based resource sponsored by a private company of the same name, offers access to articles and journals. DeepDyve states that its goal is to serve people who are unaffiliated with institutions. It can be searched for content as a database and returns results with author, title, source, a line about the purpose of the article, and the cost to access. Holdings can also be browsed by subject, journal title, and publisher. Selecting a journal title brings up all of its contents by volume and issue including the full run of many titles. Access to an article lasts seven days. Printing is limited to selected publishers. Fee-based resources are, by definition, part of the Invisible Web. *Tags: dynamic content, fee-based*

DOAJ: DIRECTORY OF OPEN ACCESS JOURNALS

www.doaj.org

This resource offers access to full-text articles from online scholarly publications covering all subjects. While it calls itself a directory, DOAJ is really a database of articles that can be searched using keywords. A browsing option permits users to search journals by subject area or to go directly to specific titles. The collection includes titles from many countries. The website includes a statement about the selection criteria, which favor research and scientific publications. DOAJ is maintained by Lund University in Lund, Sweden; the service is financed by sponsors and members. Many of the journals and articles represented in DOAJ may be found using Google Scholar, but here they are presented in an organized and easily accessed manner. The ability to see a whole collection of scholarly titles at once through the directory is an advantage that brings this tool into the Invisible Web family. *Tags: dynamic content*

BASE—BIELEFELD ACADEMIC SEARCH ENGINE

www.base-search.net

BASE is sponsored by the Bielefeld University Library in Bielefeld, Germany. This fine search engine has the specific goal of covering material not readily found by commercial search engines. It seeks to include "intellectually selected resources" that meet academic quality standards and "web resources of the 'Deep Web,' which are ignored by commercial search engines or get lost in the vast quantity of hits." Materials searched include over 30 million documents in several languages. Options include full-text, author, title, and subject searches. The collection can also be browsed by Dewey Decimal Classification (DDC) or document type. Searches can then be refined by author, subject, DDC, year of publication, language, content provider, and document type. The search record includes all this information as well as URLs, publishers, journal names, and other descriptive information. *Tags: unique resources not found or linked to elsewhere*

TECHXTRA: ENGINEERING, MATHEMATICS, AND COMPUTING
www.techxtra.ac.uk

TechXtra is a free service that, according to the site, focuses on "articles, books, the best websites, the latest industry news, job announcements, technical reports, technical data, full text e-prints, the latest research, thesis [*sic*] & dissertations, teaching and learning resources and more, in engineering, mathematics and computing." Developed and sponsored by Heriot Watt University, in Edinburgh, Scotland, TechXtra states that it searches parts of the web that Google does not or, as they describe it, the "Hidden Web." TechXtra lists the collections that it searches relevant to engineering, mathematics, and computing, including content from over fifty publishers and providers. Basic and advanced keyword searching are available. Search produces a list of resources identifying how many items were found by collection and indicating whether full text is available. Selecting a resource result brings up specific information: title and author information, abstract, and a link to full text. TechXtra always lists clearly whether full text is available and, if not, provides a link to the publisher's site for purchase if that is desired. Where full text is not available through TechXtra, users may be able to get access through the subscription-based services for which their institution has already paid. Users can also go directly to individual collections/resources to find descriptions of resources and links. Extras include guides, industry reports, and job leads. *Tags: unique resources not found or linked to elsewhere, vertical*

CITESEERX
http://citeseerx.ist.psu.edu

Sponsored by the College of Information Sciences and Technology at Pennsylvania State University, CiteSeerX is a search engine that concentrates on computer and information science literature. It also provides resources on algorithms, data, metadata, services, techniques, and software that can be used to promote digital libraries. The user can search under documents, authors, and tables. Search results offer titles, source, authors, abstract, year, and number of times that the document has been cited by the other resources in the database. The users can click on the cited-by references to see those resources as well. Clicking on the title brings up an abstract, a list of citations used in the document, and link to full text. An author search brings up name and number of citations in CiteSeerX with links to documents. A table search locates documents with tabular information on a topic, then provides the usual linking information. The nature of the content makes this an Invisible Web tool. *Tags: unique resources not found or linked to elsewhere*

SCITATION
http://scitation.aip.org
Sponsored by the American Institute of Physics, the world's largest publisher of physics journals, this database offers all things physics. The journals can be browsed by title, publisher, and subject category. Keyword searching is also available, as are advanced searching capabilities. Browsing titles brings up listings, links, and availability of full text. Most journals are open access but a limited number of titles are freely available only to members/subscribers; however, anyone can purchase articles from those publications. The site also offers professional services such as a MyScitation feature and current-awareness services that alert users to newly published information. Users can find some of the individual publications on the web if they know what to look for. What Scitation provides is indexing across many publications at once, including fee-based Invisible Web resources. *Tags: fee-based, unique resources not found or linked to elsewhere*

CITEULIKE: EVERYONE'S LIBRARY
www.citeulike.org
CiteULike is a social bookmarking site sponsored by Oversity Ltd., a British company. It labels itself as intended for the collection of "scholarly references." Users can become members of the CiteULike community and use it to organize and maintain their bookmarks. However, even nonmembers can search the references to get leads to articles about a subject. The articles are linked and identified by who posted them and when. They become a sort of recommendations list that might appeal to some researchers; because the references are linked, CiteULike functions also as a resource discovery tool. It is not a search engine; its results lists are the product of a community

building resources. The search results may be findable elsewhere, but without the unique community endorsement. *Tags: unique material not found or linked to elsewhere*

THIRD LAYER: EVEN MORE SPECIALIZED TOOLS

Finally, there is a layer of research tools for people engaged in very specialized fields. Here are some examples of what the Invisible Web has to offer them.

E-PRINT NETWORK—ENERGY, SCIENCE, AND TECHNOLOGY FOR THE RESEARCH COMMUNITY

www.osti.gov/eprints

The E-Print Network offers scientific and technology-related resources collected from over 35,000 databases worldwide, including materials on basic and applied sciences, physics, chemistry, biology and life sciences, materials science, nuclear sciences and engineering, energy research, and computer and information technologies. Keyword search results include title, author, date, a summary, and the source of the item, where a link to the item can be found. Full-text availability depends on the source. Real-time searching shows the results being compiled at the time of query. The advanced search function shows all the contributing collections, which can then be searched separately if desired. There is also a "browse by discipline" function: selecting a discipline brings up an alphabetical list of authors and contributors with their affiliation. Clicking on a name directs the user to that individual's website. Users can also search scientific societies by discipline and language. *Tags: format, unique content not found or linked to elsewhere*

PLANTS DATABASE

http://plants.usda.gov

An example of a specialized database, sponsored by the United States Department of Agriculture, Natural Conservation Services, this database has one focus: anything to do with plants. A user can search under the common or scientific name of a plant, by characteristics, by region, and more. The Plants Database is a very reliable source and, like many government resources, its content forms part of the Invisible web. *Tags: dynamic content, niche*

THE LABYRINTH: RESOURCES FOR MEDIEVAL STUDIES

http://labyrinth.georgetown.edu

Sponsored by Georgetown University in Washington, DC, the Labyrinth is an example of a specialized directory on a single theme, medieval studies. Directories require the user to select from broad subject categories and browse the offered content. Often, directories have several layers of increasingly specific subject topics to select. The Labyrinth website offers broad category listings, narrower categories, and subcategories. Selecting a category brings up links to digitized resources that may include images, primary texts, maps, course materials, discussion lists and forums, and more. Keyword searching is an additional option. *Tags: unique content not found or linked to elsewhere, niche*

FOLD 3: THE WEB'S PREMIER COLLECTION OF ORIGINAL MILITARY RECORDS

www.fold3.com

This tool searches United States military records and can help historians, genealogists, and families learn more about those who have served. The database covers all American wars from the Revolutionary War through the Vietnam War and offers photographs and digitized records. It was developed by Footnote.com. *Tags: dynamic content, niche*

FINDSOUNDS: SEARCH THE WEB FOR SOUNDS

http://findsounds.com

FindSounds claims to be the only search engine devoted to finding sound effects on the web. It offers searching in several languages, including English, German, French, and Chinese, among others. Searching for a sound using textual description or approximation produces a list of sources of the sound which can be downloaded and listened to, along with information on file type and properties. As an example, a search under cat found over 200 cat sounds. The search also offers to find similar sounds. FindSounds is free, offers a mobile app, FindSounds Mobile, and is one of those unusual sources for unusual needs. It prides itself on being able to find sources not available through Google and other major search engines and provides a comparison of its results with theirs. FindSounds was developed by Comparisonics Corporation. *Tags: formats*

YOVISTO: ACADEMIC VIDEO SEARCH

http://yovisto.com

Yovisto is a video search engine specializing in educational video content, including online lectures. A search returns video screenshots and titles, duration, number of views, and other information, along with a link to each video and related subject tags that are in turn linked. Yovisto utilizes semantic search, so that the "user has not only access to keyword-based search results, but will also be guided by content-based associations to enable serendipitous discovery" (Waitelonis and Sack 2011, 646). Clicking on a video selection brings up more specific information, including description and institutional affiliation. The user can also browse under "lectures" and by universities and speakers. Yovisto.com is a private search company. *Tags: formats*

FINDTHATFILE: FINDS WHAT NOBODY ELSE DOES

www.findthatfile.com

FindThatFile claims to be the most extensive file search tool on the Internet, covering forty-seven file types. Google's advanced search only offers ten. A search can be conducted for all file types, or the user can select from documents, videos, audio files, fonts, software, or compressed file formats. Search results include a breakdown of formats by document type (PDF, text [TXT], PowerPoint [PPT], etc.), audio format (e.g., MP3), and so forth. Results can be downloaded and show date and size of files. The site claims to screen out malware and viruses. *Tags: formats, unique materials not found or linked to elsewhere*

SLIDEFINDER: FINDING YOU THE RIGHT SLIDES

www.slidefinder.net

SlideFinder is a search engine that looks only at PowerPoint presentations to locate materials. A user can search for ideas or download entire presentations, which are offered in English, French, Spanish, and other languages. Much of this material is university based, and the searcher can even look by name of institution to find resources. *Tags: formats*

HATHITRUST DIGITAL LIBRARY

www.Hathitrust.org

The HathiTrust organization refers to itself as "a collaboration of major research institutions and libraries working to ensure that the cultural record is preserved and accessible long into the future." At present, it has sixty partners who are making digital collections available through the repository. It offers over 700 collections so far, from universities and libraries. Its partners include schools such as of the University of California, Columbia University, and Cornell University, and libraries such as the Library of Congress, the New York Public Library, and Yale University Library. Collections can be searched in three ways: catalog search, full-text search, and browse. Copyright restrictions are noted for items that cannot be offered in full text, along with links to help locate the item in the member organizations or elsewhere. *Tags: dynamic content, federated search*

MAKING OF AMERICA
http://quod.lib.umich.edu/m/moagrp

The Making of America Project has been a long-term effort to create a digital collection of primary documents related to American history. It is a collaborative endeavor among libraries, principally the University of Michigan Library and the Cornell University Library. It is possible to browse through the alphabetical list of the collections, which vary vastly in size. Topics vary from space flight to rocks and minerals to Harriet Beecher Stowe. *Tags: dynamic content, unique content not found or linked to elsewhere*

SOCIAL SCIENCE RESEARCH NETWORK
www.ssrn.com

The Social Science Research Network (SSRN) is a worldwide collaborative sponsored by Social Science Electronic Publishing, Inc. The site, which supports dissemination of social science research, offers nearly half a million scholarly abstracts and nearly as many full-text papers. Its network covers subject areas such as accounting and other business fields, music, philosophy, literature, politics, and more. A user can research papers by subject and author. The results list shows title, author, publication information, when the item was posted and last revised, number of viewings, links, abstract, and full-text access. Many of the research papers presented are preprints. The user can also browse subject networks for papers. Subscribers receive added benefits. *Tags: unique materials not found or linked to elsewhere*

Some may argue that the selection of Invisible Web tools represented here (and summarized in table 6.3) overlooks other valuable resources, and that is probably true. These tools are only a sampling of the riches of the Invisible Web. Every researcher is encouraged to create a personal list of such valuable tools.

TABLE 6.3

Subject breakdown for Invisible Web tools

Academic	BASE
Business	BizNar
General and popular interest	HathiTrust, Pipl, Scout.me, Yummly
Health and medicine	MedNar
Internet and technology	CiteSeerX, Internet Archives, TechXtra
Journals	DeepDyve, DOAJ
Literature and humanities	Voice of the Shuttle
Media and graphics	New York Public Library Digital Collection, Yovisto
News	Popurls
Science	E-Print Network, Plants Database, Scitation, WorldWideScience.org
Social media	CiteULike, Social Mention, Social Sciences Research Network, Topsy
Social sciences	Making of America, Fold3, Labyrinth
Special formats	FindSounds, FindThatFile, SlideFinder
Statistics	Data.gov

REFERENCES

Devine, Jane, and Francine Egger-Sider. 2009. *Going Beyond Google: The Invisible Web in Learning and Teaching*. New York: Neal-Schuman.

Ogg, Erica. 2011. "Yummly's Semantic Recipe Search Gets Spicy." *GigaOM* (blog), August 24. http://gigaom.com/2011/08/24/yummlys-semantic-recipe -search-gets-spicy.

Waitelonis, Jörg, and Harald Sack. 2011. "Toward Exploratory Video Search Using Linked Data." *Multimedia Tools and Applications*, no. 59, no. 2: 645–672. http://dx.doi.org/10.1007/s11042-011-0733-1.

THE FUTURE OF THE INVISIBLE WEB AND ITS IMPLICATIONS FOR TEACHING

THE FUTURE OF THE INVISIBLE WEB IS INEXTRICA-bly tied to search. The boundary between the surface web and the Invisible Web has always been a moving target, as each search engine creates its own Invisible Web by the ever-changing decisions it makes as to what gets included or excluded from a results list. In addition, as search engines become more and more sophisticated with advances in technology, the boundaries between these webs, surface and deep, visible and invisible, move elastically in new directions. This chapter will examine technological trends newly on the horizon and how these changes in search intersect with the Invisible Web. These trends include human intervention, natural language searching, social networking, personalization, the Semantic Web, and mobile apps. Each of these trends will affect and be affected by information literacy instruction. A study of these trends will answer the question of whether the Invisible Web is a concept that web users still need to consider. Does the Invisible Web retain a significance that makes it an important element of information literacy instruction?

OVERVIEW

A literature search provides a few insights into forthcoming changes to search. The focus of this book is the Invisible Web—broadly defined as everything on the web that is not found by general-purpose search engines. Therefore, any tweak or change in search technology affects the fluid boundary between the visible and Invisible Web. It thus behooves us to highlight changes in how web users will conduct searches. Marti A. Hearst, a professor at the School of Information at the University of California, Berkeley, and author of *Search User Interfaces*, sums up what the future holds for web users: "Users will speak rather than type, watch video rather than read, and use technology socially rather than alone" (Hearst 2011, 60). She elaborates further: "Today, there is a notable trend toward more 'natural' user interfaces: pointing with fingers rather than mice, speaking rather than typing, viewing videos rather than reading text, and writing full sentences rather than artificial keywords" (60). Thus one of the major changes affecting users will be the ability to speak queries; voice commands are already gaining ground in nonacademic settings with Apple's Siri and Voice Search on Google, among a host of similar applications.

Being able to speak a request for information on road construction, for example, is probably easier for users than finding the correct keywords: what type of road, in what country, under what conditions, and so forth. If the technology gets savvy enough to support a true conversation, then it is to be hoped that users might eventually be steered toward Invisible Web content. Oren Etzioni, professor of computer science and engineering at the University of Washington, advocates for more natural interfaces in web searching—natural language searching and answering. He senses a paradigm shift from information retrieval to question answering. Instead of retrieving a long list of results to pore through, a user will simply obtain the answer to the question posed. For Etzioni, the challenge is as follows: "Moving up the information food chain requires a search engine that can interpret a user's question, extract facts from all the information on the web, and select an appropriate answer" (Etzioni 2011, 25). The IBM computer Watson embodies the future of search, with its knowledge equal to the content of more than one million books. In a famous test, Watson competed with human contestants in a game of *Jeopardy* and won. The machine could interpret natural language queries and return answers in a very timely fashion. Watson's advanced technology exemplifies Oren Etzioni's assertion that the future of search lies in the ability of natural language not just to ask questions but also to answer them (Etzioni 2011). This type of searching depends on Semantic Web technologies, which insert meaning into search operations and return more precise and relevant result lists.

Search is also going mobile, with apps often replacing web browsers. According to one research firm, by 2015 access to the Internet through mobile devices in the United States will surpass access through PCs (International Data Corporation 2011). Database publishers in conjunction with libraries need to be more active in offering database access on smartphones and other mobile devices. These apps will directly affect access to Invisible Web content.

Another change, already in the wings, is that search is turning more and more social, whether through collaboration using appropriate tools, reliance on others through networks such as Facebook, or contributions toward a greater goal as in the phenomenon of crowdsourcing (Hearst 2011, 62–64). In an interview on *Memeburn*, Nelson Mattos, a Google vice president, explains that the direction search is taking is local as well as more personalized and that social ranking will become part of search results (Atagana 2011). This integration is already taking place with Google's new networking platform Google+ and in the partnership between the search engine Bing and Facebook.

Nowadays, users seek out a great deal of content through video, as the explosion of YouTube attests. Alexa, a company that monitors Internet activity, ranks YouTube in third place after Facebook and Google in terms of traffic (www.alexa.com/topsites, as of 2013). Libraries, academic and other, have been responding by creating videos that explain how to use a library, how to obtain an article through interlibrary loan, how to use a particular database, and more. But the major development in this area is online video sharing, which takes place through social media such as Facebook. The value of library-produced video expands mightily when students can recommend videos to each other describing, say, the use of a specialized database relating to an assignment.

How would such changes affect the use of the Invisible Web? The ability to speak queries into a mobile device and receive ready-made answers in an academic setting might perhaps steer students toward more Invisible Web content for research if the apps operate as niche tools. More and more apps are being developed for subscription databases—for example,

EBSCOhost, AccessMyLibrary from Gale, ArXiv, and WorldCat Mobile. If a student could simply ask a database app using natural language rather than rigid keyword search strings to locate ten articles on a particular topic and have the results pop up on a mobile device, the use of these databases might go up exponentially! The sharing of resources among peers, between teachers and students, and among researchers in a specific field is becoming a critical factor in the process of obtaining information. The lynchpin remains the teaching of information literacy, for if users do not know about the existence of highly relevant, structured databases in their fields, then all the sharing in the world will not lead them to the appropriate information. Teaching all users—students, everyday life researchers, and professionals— about the existence of specialized information not readily available through general-purpose search engines is an important task for all educators, librarians, high school teachers, and college faculty. Teaching the Invisible Web will ensure that researchers will find and use its rich but elusive content.

RETURN TO HUMAN-POWERED SEARCH

Various elements seem to converge on the idea that search has made a 360-degree turn and is headed, once again, in the direction of human control. After many years of searches performed exclusively by information professionals, followed by the advent of the World Wide Web, which was created as a completely disintermediated environment, search is making a slow return to human intervention. Carol Tenopir called Dialog, operational since the late sixties, "the grandfather of online database systems" (2008, 26). Dialog was costly and difficult to use but it was in heavy demand; only information professionals could use it, and they required specialized training. In libraries, special, public, and academic, researchers required librarians to conduct the searches that would answer their reference questions. There was always an intermediary, the information professional, between the user and the answer.

This paradigm shifted in 1991 with the advent of the World Wide Web, which allowed direct access to information. Suddenly anyone and everyone could type words into a search box and obtain results. The amount of information available through the web grew to the point that users were soon overwhelmed by the number of results each search generated.

"Information overload" became a leitmotiv and led to a greater emphasis in academic libraries on the evaluation of sources. It remains the case that students usually do not go beyond the first page of search engine results, effectively making all other results invisible. Students also feel that whatever Google pulls up is "good enough"—they have no incentive to search out better but invisible (to them) resources.

The era of disintermediation in searching was challenged in the early 2000s, when social networking as we know it today took off. "Friends" now enter the equation when it comes to sharing information. The academic realm still lags behind the everyday and purely social aspects of social networking but it has brought the human element back into search. Social media, as an antidote to information overload, has moved search from an individual pursuit to a social one. The Invisible Web is intermittently visible in social networking sites: some Invisible Web information is sometimes available through Google and Bing searches. The Invisible Web will have changed dimensions if structured and specialized databases become mobile and accessible through social networking sites.

TOOLS

The movement back toward human authority and away from reliance on robotic searching is small and underfunded. Projects such as The Librarian's Index to the Internet, a directory compiled by librarians in California, or Intute, a website of sources for study and research created in England, have been abandoned due to lack of financial support. Reference Extract, a project planned by OCLC and the information schools at Syracuse University and the University of Washington with the goal of making it easier to find reliable information, seems never to have gotten off the ground.

But more search tools seem to be experimenting with human intervention. The search engine Blekko (http://blekko.com) relies on slashtag filters to narrow searches and uses expert evaluation in certain subject areas. Wolfram|Alpha (www.wolframalpha.com) calls itself a "computational knowledge engine": it "computes" answers to queries based on its own database. As its home page explains, "Wolfram|Alpha uses built-in knowledge curated by human experts to compute on the fly a specific answer and analysis for every query." It operates more like a database than a search engine and offers access to Invisible Web content primarily of a numerical or statistical nature. An example: When did

Whitney Houston die? Wolfram|Alpha simply provides the answer: Saturday, February 11, 2012. Google provides a list of results in which the user has to find the answer. A fee-based version, Wolfram|Alpha Pro, was launched in 2012. According to a February 6, 2012, *New York Times* article, Wolfram|Alpha now handles a quarter of the answers for Siri, Apple's voice-activated mobile software tool (Lohr 2012), often with Invisible Web content. Academic Index (www.academicindex.net) is yet another tool which is adding humans to the search process. Created by the former chair of the Texas Association of School Librarians, this metasearch engine draws from databases and resources approved by librarians and educators.

Ask-an-expert sites are also examples of human-powered search tools. Although these sites rely heavily on tools such as Google, the fact that a human being looks up the answer to a query makes it possible that Invisible Web content is also being accessed by such sites. According to the OCLC study *Perceptions of Libraries, 2010*, which we have cited elsewhere in this book, the use of online reference increased dramatically since its previous report in 2005. What is especially intriguing is that ask-an-expert sites nearly tripled in use among the general population (from 15% to 43%) compared to ask-a-librarian sites, which saw only a 2% increase over the same time period. The greatest jump in use of these ask-a-question sites was among young adults (De Rosa et al. 2010, 33–34).

COACH

An October 3, 2011, article in the *New Yorker* by a surgeon offers the idea that just as top athletes and singers all have coaches, everyone else should, too (Gawande 2011). The author goes on to explain that, after many years of working as a surgeon, he felt that he had hit a plateau in the operating room, and in order to move beyond that stage, he needed someone to observe him, shadow him, and critique him; in other words, he needed a coach. Not everyone is ready to put him- or herself in such a vulnerable position, but this idea could easily be transferred to the world of searching.

Just as a drama coach or a football coach can improve an actor's or player's performance by breaking it down to analyze every element individually, so a search coach can help students by analyzing their searching habits. The student or the everyday life researcher could benefit from a coach who can, after observing how these users conduct their respective searches, show them new tricks, moving them profitably beyond their comfort zones. That is already the function of the reference interview: an information professional has the student re-create a search, then pushes the envelope by asking that user to rephrase the keyword search with new terminology or conduct a similar search in a completely different database. In a November 6, 2011, *New York Times* article, Jaywon Choe describes the use of personal librarians for students at several universities, including Drexel, Barnard, and Yale. These "personal librarians" help students narrow or broaden their topics, look for appropriate databases, and locate and use information effectively. Such, indeed, was the mandate of information literacy as presented in 1989 in the final report of the American Library Association's Presidential Committee on Information Literacy (American Library Association 1989). The human element is what resonates in these scenarios: in order to become better researchers, it behooves everyone to find a coach, a teacher, a librarian who can sharpen skills and make users more proficient and confident at conducting research.

Why is this idea of a research coach part of an analysis of the future of the Invisible Web? Chapter 2 concluded with a quote by Stephen Arnold, a well-known search specialist, who suggested that web search was, after many years of being based purely on algorithms, once again becoming dependent on social and human mediation. The coach is the teacher and, in this case, the librarian has to teach like a coach. A librarian will, if at all possible, use relevant data to answer queries, whether the information falls within visible or invisible content. The likelihood that databases will be used is greater if a librarian/coach is involved.

SOCIAL MEDIA

As was discussed in chapter 2, users of social networking sites value and rely on the opinions of others, including family and friends. This dependence on others is being transported into search engines. John Battelle, an expert on the web, writes in his *Searchlog* on January 16, 2012: "I believe the dominant search paradigm—that of crawling a free and open web, then displaying the best results for any particular query—has been broken by the rise of Facebook on the one hand, and the app economy on the other. Both of these developments are driven by personalization—the rise of 'social.'" Social networking sites such as Facebook and Google+, on the one hand, and search engines, on the other, are playing a cat-and-mouse game to see who will prevail as users' first point of entry to conduct searches. Search and social are becoming integrated into one entity. Facebook has its own search engine, Graph Search, thus firmly blending these two elements and, possibly, representing a new vision of the future of search. Bing has been integrating Facebook "Like" data into its results lists since October 2010 (Sterling 2011). And a Bing blog post announced on May 16, 2011, that "today, Bing is bringing the collective IQ of the Web together with the opinions of the people you trust most, to bring the 'Friend Effect' to search." Google+ responded by introducing "Search, plus Your World," so that results from Google+ will be incorporated into Google results lists. "A US study into 'social login' habits has added to increasing evidence that Google+ is the second most popular online social network, after Facebook" (Worrall 2013). Facebook and Google+ are trying to become one-stop searching portals for everyone. Of course, the underlying reason for this goal is to obtain more data about users and, as a result, more advertising revenue.

These changes could result in research also entering the social arena: students will first log on to Facebook or Google+, then conduct the research for their assignments. The results of such searches will include websites and documents that their friends like or recommend. Information within Facebook has hitherto been part of the Invisible Web, but there is now a fine and ever-shifting line between the surface and Invisible Web. The "walled garden," as Stephen Arnold has labeled Facebook (2010, 20), seems to be opening its doors wider and wider. Will students eventually have access to Invisible Web content through their Facebook and Google+ accounts? Potentially, students could receive recommendations from friends regarding which resources to use for a particular research assignment and then which results to look at within these particular sources.

The issue to be addressed by information professionals in this new social search era is the place of authority in research. If students steer each other toward sources within databases where the material has already been vetted, then social search will be a boon for users in general, students in particular. However, if students recommend to each other sources culled only from the surface web, then the future of research will be seriously and negatively affected. Just because several friends "like" a particular source that they found on Bing after logging onto Facebook does not necessarily make that source valuable or reliable. A critical mass of research "likes" does not make the research right!

As access to information gets more extensive and chaotic, people seek to operate within a community of peers they can trust, peers who can offer feedback in their disciplines. Hence the rise of professional communities such as the Social Science Research Network (SSRN), which brings together specialists in similar fields. SSRN allows early dissemination of research, through abstracts or working papers, and rapid feedback from other scholars which can then be incorporated into a revised and, eventually, a final version. This type of community network breaks down some barriers to research, previously available only within subscriptions. Another example, on a much smaller scale, of such a closed community within the confines of the Invisible Web is the CUNY Technical Services wiki created and maintained by the Technical Services librarians of the City University of New York. This wiki contains information about best practices for acquisitions and cataloging, papers on new cataloging rules and other developments, and important articles from relevant literature. Other examples of such communities have been given in chapter 2.

Thus social media will have a mixed effect on the use of the Invisible Web. Once social media are used as search tools, result lists will tend to link to the same ten "likes," eventually defeating the purpose of obtaining a personal recommendation from a friend. Nonetheless, social media could work to drive users *away* from the Invisible Web. It is far easier to ask a friend to recommend an article on a particular topic than to venture into an unknown database. On the other hand, the notion of the Invisible Web takes on a new dimension within social media, depending on privacy settings: information within a closed group is part of the Invisible Web.

PERSONALIZATION

The development of social searching accentuates another trend, which will only get more pronounced with time—the phenomenon of personalization, already addressed in chapter 2. Personalization captures and uses personal data such that no two people conducting a search on a general-purpose search engine will obtain the same results. With the inclusion of personal information within search results, the information silos that Eli Pariser warns of in his book *The Filter Bubble* will become even more ubiquitous. Chapter 2 addressed this problem in greater detail. The evaluation of sources will become a more complex operation for students. Objective, unbiased sources will be harder to find in the mix of social results.

In order to reclaim their online privacy, a growing number of web users are switching search engines because they object to the way Google and others track their every move, logging their search terms for posterity.

Major search engines track users' IP addresses and install cookies on computers to track search terms, day and time of search, and links followed. A newer search engine named DuckDuckGo does not track search information and thus prevents the sharing or selling of such information. It refers to such sharing as "search leakage" (https://duckduckgo.com/privacy.html). Ixquick is another search engine that does not keep personal data. Its tagline is "the world's most private search engine" (https://www.ixquick.com).

SEMANTIC WEB

Tim Berners-Lee, the father of the World Wide Web, defined the Semantic Web in 2001 as "not a separate Web but an extension of the current one, in which information is given well-defined meaning, better enabling computers and people to work in cooperation" (Berners-Lee, Hendler, and Lassila 2001). The evolution of the web has gone from linking web pages in Web 1.0, to linking people in Web 2.0 (the social web), to linking data in Web 3.0, also known as the Semantic Web (Doszkocs 2010, 36). "The Semantic Web allows computers to *understand the meaning* of information as opposed to simply displaying information" (Morris 2011, 43). It seeks to establish better finding methods than the algorithms presently used by general-purpose search engines so that it can give more targeted answers to queries.

Research in this field is ongoing: Semantic Web techniques already operate within general search engines such as Hakia and Bing, specialized search engines such as HealthMash, databases such as LexisNexis and PubMed, and library catalogs such as the one at North Carolina State University. Some of the characteristics of the Semantic Web already in place include faceted clustering in library catalogs and databases, results that show up before the user finishes typing (as with Google Instant), and the combining of vertical semantic search, federated search, and various types of content and topic clusters (as on HealthMash) (Doszkocs 2010, 42).

How will the Semantic Web interface with the Invisible Web? Ideally, the Semantic Web will reduce the number of silos of information users must access in order to obtain useful answers to their queries. As many information silos reside in the Invisible Web, searching the Semantic Web should tap databases that offer users a richer array of valuable sources. The end result is summarized by Michael A. Keller, University Librarian at

Stanford University: "Semantic Web approaches . . . offer new opportunities for addressing the traditional and prevailing problems of too many silos of content, too many disparate modes of search and access, and too little precision and too much ambiguity in search results in the extreme environments of academic information resources" (Keller 2011, 11). But the job of creating the ontologism, the system of relationships between words and ideas, needed to map the web is massive and only partially underway. Without this background work, the Semantic Web remains a goal in the future.

APPS

In their now famous *Wired* article "The Web is Dead, Long Live the Internet," Chris Anderson and Michael Wolff make the case that "for the sake of the optimized experience on mobile devices, users forgo the general-purpose browser. They use the Net, but not the Web. Fast beats flexible." Some fee-based apps, which are in effect niche tools, are part of the Invisible Web, and their use is growing exponentially to the detriment of browsers. It is more about getting and less about searching. An app allows users to go straight to desired sites without wasting time opening a browser and typing in a URL. Thus, as one sector of the Invisible Web becomes visible, another segment seems to move over to the invisible side. What matters is that web users look up from their specialized apps, their Google searches, or their conversations on Facebook to ask themselves whether the research tool at hand is appropriate for a particular inquiry or whether other tools should be considered. Effective search cannot limit itself to one silo, no matter what the resource, the technology, the tool used. Users must place search within an informational context and evaluate the transaction that has taken place and what still needs to be done to make it complete.

CONCLUSION

There will always be a need for subscription databases with their structured data offering access to specialized, general, and academic sources. For the near future, this content will continue to reside entirely in the Invisible Web as introduced in its traditional, more technological definition outlined in chapter 1. On the cognitive level, the solution to insufficient awareness and use of the Invisible Web remains education. Whatever the information and however it arrives—as text or as speech, via PC or smartphone, tablet, or some yet unknown new interface—the key issue remains the same: How does the user know where the information came from and how accurate it is? Evaluation remains the key to effective information search; this holds true for visible or Invisible Web content. Information literacy—the ability to locate, use, and evaluate information—remains critical. Is the return to human intervention in search a positive phenomenon? In some cases, yes: if searching gets increasingly harder as more and more material is thrown into the mix of results, users, students, or anyone conducting searches may veer back toward seeking help from information professionals. In other cases, no: the flood of personalized tidbits could deter users from getting objective information about a topic. A coach, a mentor, a librarian will be needed to help separate the wheat from the chaff. The Invisible Web remains a moving target but generally provides more specialized, appropriate sources for users. As the information world becomes more chaotic, more overwhelming, it behooves students to zero in on such sources. But the ultimate lesson to be learned is to apply evaluative criteria to any source, wherever it may come from.

REFERENCES

American Library Association. 1989. *Presidential Committee on Information Literacy: Final Report.* www.ala.org/acrl/publications/whitepapers/presidential.

Anderson, Chris, and Michael Wolff. 2010. "The Web Is Dead, Long Live the Internet." *Wired*, September. www.wired.com/magazine/2010/08/ff_webrip/all/1.

Arnold, Stephen E. 2010. "Is a Search Revolution Brewing?" *Information Today* 27, no. 6: 20–21. Academic Search Complete.

Atagana, Michelle. 2011. "The Future of Search Is Social: Q&A with Google's Nelson Mattos." *Memeburn*, December 7. http://memeburn.com/2011/12/the-future-of-search-is-social-qa-with-googles-nelson-mattos/.

Battelle, John. 2012. "What Might a Facebook Search Engine Look Like?" *John Battelle's Searchblog*, January 16. http://battellemedia.com/archives/2012/01/what-might-a-facebook-search-engine-look-like.php.

Berners-Lee, Tim, James Hendler, and Ora Lassila. 2001. "The Semantic Web." *Scientific American* 284, no. 5: 34–43. General Science Full Text (H. W. Wilson).

Bing Team. 2011. "Facebook Friends Now Fueling Faster Decisions on Bing." *Search Blog*, May 16. www.bing.com/community/site_blogs/b/search/ archive/2011/05/16/news-announcement-may-17.aspx.

Choe, Jaywon. 2011. "My Own Private Librarian." *New York Times*, November 4. www.nytimes.com/2011/11/06/education/edlife/my-own-private-librarian.html.

De Rosa, Cathy, Joanne Cantrell, Matthew Carlson, Peggy Gallagher, Janet Hawk, and Charlotte Sturtz. 2010. *Perceptions of Libraries, 2010: Context and Community—a Report to the OCLC Membership*. Dublin, OH: OCLC.

Doszkocs, Tamas. 2010. "Semantic Search Engines Mean Well." *Online* 34, no. 4: 36–42. Academic Search Complete.

Etzioni, Oren. 2011. "Search Needs a Shake-Up." *Nature* 476, no. 7358: 25–26. http://dx.doi.org/10.1038/476025a.

Gawande, Atul. 2011. "Personal Best: Top Athletes and Singers Have Coaches: Should You?" *New Yorker*, October 3. www.newyorker.com/reporting/2011/ 10/03/111003fa_fact_gawande.

Hearst, Marti A. 2009. *Search User Interfaces*. Cambridge: Cambridge University Press.

——. 2011. "'Natural' Search User Interfaces." *Communications of the ACM* 54, no. 11: 60–67. http://dx.doi.org/10.1145/2018396.2018414.

International Data Corporation (IDC). 2011. "IDC: More Mobile Internet Users Than Wireline Users in the U.S. by 2015." Press release, IDC.com, September 12. www.idc.com/getdoc.jsp?containerId=prUS23028711.

Keller, Michael A. 2011. "Linked Data: A Way Out of the Information Chaos and toward the Semantic Web." *EDUCAUSE Review* 46, no. 4: 10–11. www.educause.edu/ero/ article/linked-data-way-out-information-chaos-and-toward-semantic-web.

Lohr, Steve. 2012. "Wolfram, a Search Engine, Finds Answers Within Itself." *New York Times*, February 6. www.nytimes.com/2012/02/07/technology/wolfram -a-search-engine-finds-answers-within-itself.html.

Morris, Robin D. 2011. "Web 3.0: Implications for Online Learning." *TechTrends* 55, no. 1: 42–46. http://dx.doi.org/10.1007/s11528-011-0469-9.

Pariser, Eli. 2011. *The Filter Bubble: What the Internet Is Hiding from You*. New York: Penguin.

Sterling, Greg. 2011. "Bing Ups Ante in Social Search, Adds More Facebook 'Likes' to Search Results." *Search Engine Land* (blog), May 16. http://searchengineland. com/bing-ups-ante-in-social-search-re-ranking-serps-with-likes-77269.

Tenopir, Carol. 2008. "Dialog Finds a New Home." *Library Journal* 133, no. 14: 26. Library, Information Science & Technology Abstracts with Full Text.

Worrall, JJ. 2013. "'Monster' Google+ Catching Up with Social Rivals." *Irish Times*, July 18. www.irishtimes.com/business/sectors/technology/monster-google-catching-up-with-social-rivals-1.1466531.

APPENDIX

SURVEYMONKEY SURVEY
Invisible Web/Deep Web/Hidden Web

This survey was approved by the City University of New York (CUNY) Institutional Review Board (IRB) (Certificate 11-05-0010-0139, dated June 6, 2011).

Question 1: Do you know about the Invisible Web?
- ☐ yes
- ☐ no

Question 2: If not, do you want to know more?
- ☐ yes
- ☐ no

Question 3: How would you define the Invisible Web?

Question 4: Have you used it in your own research?
- ☐ yes
- ☐ no

Question 5: How did you learn about the Invisible Web?
- ☐ Journal articles
- ☐ Books
- ☐ Presentations (workshops)
- ☐ Course work

☐ From colleagues
☐ Other ways?

Question 6: Do you teach about the Invisible Web?
☐ yes
☐ no

Question 7: Do you think that students should be taught about the Invisible Web? Please explain why or why not.

Question 8: In what circumstances do you teach about the Invisible Web or would you teach about it if given the opportunity?
☐ One-shot class presentations
☐ Credit-bearing courses
☐ Workshops
☐ Reference desk
☐ Tutorials
☐ Other ways?

Question 9: How do you introduce the Invisible Web when teaching?

Question 10: Do you think that learning about the Invisible Web helps students with their research?

Question 11: Should every student be taught about the Invisible Web, and if so, at what grade level?

Question 12: Thanks for your participation in this survey. If you have any additional comments, please share them here.

SELECTED
ADDITIONAL READINGS

Anderson, Janna, and Lee Rainie. 2010. "The Fate of the Semantic Web." Pew Internet & American Life Project, May 4. http://pewinternet.org/Reports/2010/Semantic-Web/Overview.aspx.

Arnold, Stephen E. 2009. "Real-Time Search: Where Retrieval and Discovery Collide." *Online* 33, no. 6: 40–41. Academic Search Complete.

———. 2011. "RockMelt: Research Degrading to 'Desearch.'" *Information Today* 28, no. 2: 26. Education Research Complete.

Badke, William. 2010. "Content, Content Everywhere." *Online* 34, no. 2: 52–53. Academic Search Complete.

Barile, Lori. 2011. "Mobile Technologies for Libraries: A List of Mobile Applications and Resources for Development." *College & Research Libraries News* 72, no. 4: 222–225. Education Full Text.

Bittner, Sven, and Andre Müller. 2011. "Social Networking Tools and Research Information Systems: Do they Compete?" *Webology* 8, no. 1: 1–8. Library, Information Science & Technology Abstracts with Full Text.

Bradley, Fiona. 2009. "Discovering Linked Data." *Library Journal* 134, no. 7: 48–50. Academic Search Complete.

Choy, Fatt Cheong. 2011. "From Library Stacks to Library-in-a-Pocket: Will Users Be Around?" *Library Management* 32, no. 1/2: 62–72. http://dx.doi.org/10.1108/01435121111102584.

Cleland, Scott, and Ira Brodsky. 2011. *Search & Destroy: Why You Can't Trust Google Inc.* St. Louis: Telescope Books.

Coyle, Karen. 2009. "Making Connections." *Library Journal* 134, no. 7: 44–47. Academic Search Complete.

"The Deep Web Today: Web Government Databases." 2010. *Information Advisor* 22, no. 11: 1–4.

Drake, Miriam A. 2008. "Federated Search—One Simple Query or Simply Wishful Thinking?" *Searcher* 16, no. 7: 22–62. Academic Search Complete.

Feldman, Susan. 2011. "The Answer Machine: Are We There Yet?" *Searcher* 19, no. 1: 18–27. Academic Search Complete.

"Google vs the Invisible Web." 2009. University of Florida Smathers Education Library. www.uflib.ufl.edu/educ/videos/GOOGLEtable.pdf.

"Infographic: Exploring the Deep Web with Semantic Search." 2012. Invention-Machine (blog), September 18. http://inventionmachine.com/the-Invention -Machine-Blog/bid/90626/INFOGRAPHIC-Exploring-the-Deep-Web-with -Semantic-Search.

Klais, Brian. 2011. "Why Mobile Is Spinning Our New Invisible Web." *Search Engine Land* (blog), October 24. http://searchengineland.com/why-mobile -is-spinning-our-new-invisible-web-98109.

Mattison, David. 2010. "The Twittering of the Search World." *Searcher* 18, no. 7: 24–35. Academic Search Complete.

McClure, Randall. 2011. "WritingResearchWriting: The Semantic Web and the Future of the Research Project." *Computers and Composition* 28, no. 4: 315–326. http://dx.doi.org/10.1016/j.compcom.2011.09.003.

Pederson, Steve. 2013. "Understanding the Deep Web in 10 Minutes." BrightPlanet white paper, March 12. www.brightplanet.com/2013/03/whitepaper-under standing-the-deep-web-in-10-minutes.

Purcell, Kristen, Joanna Brenner, and Lee Rainie. 2012. "Search Engine Use 2012." Pew Internet & American Life Project. March 9. www.pewinternet.org/~/ media//Files/Reports/2012/PIP_Search_Engine_Use_2012.pdf.

Rausing, Lisbet. 2010. "Toward a New Alexandria: Imagining the Future of Libraries." *New Republic*, March 12. www.tnr.com/article/books-and-arts/ toward-new-alexandria.

Scheeren, William O. 2012. *The Hidden Web: A Sourcebook*. Santa Barbara: Librar-ies Unlimited.

Su, Mila C. 2008. "Inside the Web: A Look at Digital Libraries and the Invisible/ Deep Web." *Journal of Educational Technology Systems* 37, no. 1: 71–82. http:// dx.doi.org/10.2190/ET.37.1.f.

Sullivan, Danny. 2009. "How Search-Like Are Social Media Sites?" *Search Engine Land* (blog), January 27. http://searchengineland.com/how-search-like-social-media-16325.

"23 Types of Social Media Sites." 2010. *On Blogging Well* (blog), February 17. http://onbloggingwell.com/23-types-of-social-media-sites.

Wright, Alex. 2008. "Searching the Deep Web." *Communications of the ACM* 51, no. 10: 14–15. http://dx.doi.org/10.1145/1400181.1400187.

———. 2009. "Exploring a 'Deep Web' that Google Can't Grasp." *New York Times*, February 23. www.nytimes.com/2009/02/23/technology/internet/23search.html.

INDEX